THE
CHALLENGE

THE
CHALLENGE

WHAT CAN WE RELY ON?

45 Principles Shared in Letters to Friends

WM. JAMES LONG

INSTITUTE FOR EXCELLENCE

A 501(c)(3) Organization

©2003 by Alliance Royale, LC
2575 Mc Cabe Way
Irvine, CA 92614
(949) 442-6630
www.allianceroyale.com

ISBN #0-9727547-0-9

Printed in the United States of America

1st Printing

Design by Bookwrights Design

CONTENTS

SECTION THREE: IMPROVING YOUR RELATIONSHIPS

SECTION FOUR: MANAGING YOUR CAREER TRANSITION

SECTION FIVE: EXPLORING BUSINESS OWNERSHIP

SECTION SIX: ENVISIONING OUR MISSION FOR THE FUTURE

ABOUT THE AUTHOR

ORDER FORM

PREFACE

Several years ago, I had a traumatic experience that led me to question everything I believed I could rely on, only to discover that I could not find peace and security in that information. With all of the education and management training I had received, I still knew I lacked the answers.

However, as I experienced my own transition, which I will tell you more about in the letters to my friends that are being shared with you, I discovered that there are clearly defined principles we can apply with complete confidence. My goal in these letters is to share the principles and experiences with each one of you so that you too may benefit from them. I know that we all can rely on them because they have worked since they were developed eons ago.

I also have a very strong feeling that we have arrived at the point in time when we all must take the final step. That step is to choose if we will live our life in highest purpose, truth and love. This is the challenge that will dominate our life experience during the next century.

I am now discovering that more and more people are searching in various directions for someone or something to provide them with a feeling of security and confidence in the future. I also have observed a growing level of concern about our financial markets and the soul of our large corporations. Many of my clients are telling me that they have little confidence in our financial system. They are asking me what they should do and who they can rely on to safeguard their savings.

There are also a growing number of people in our community who are out of work or taking forced early retirement. These people are concerned about their careers as well as their financial security. Others around me are struggling with their businesses or dealing with how to develop or maintain nourishing personal relationships.

If all of these challenges were not enough to deal with, we are inching toward a period of political unrest. Clients are privately sharing their worries that our politicians are not providing effective leadership. We are indeed living in troubling times.

I know that there are times when we feel that we have not clearly found our way and that we all experience challenges in our lives. If we listen to the people around us, they reveal many of them have either no faith at all or have lost their faith. Who would have known that we would enter the 21st century in such turmoil and instability?

I trust that this collection of letters will strengthen you and assist you in finding greater peace and happiness in your life. I also hope they will provide you with information to improve your personal effectiveness, and strengthen the management of your relationships, your finances, your businesses and your career. I am also sharing principles that will support you in your own personal growth.

I look forward to writing again soon and welcome your letters should you which to share anything with me. You may reach me via email at thechallenge@allianceroyale.com.

James

Wm. James Long

INTRODUCTION

Dear Reader,

You are very fortunate, for what took me years to discover, you will find in a matter of hours by reading this book.

THE CHALLENGE is for seekers. It's for people who have it all, but sense there is something still missing in their lives. It's also for people who don't have it, but really want it. And it's for people who are not sure what they want; they just know they have the desire to seek until they find it. As you read these stories, keep your heart open, and just listen to the words and you will know what to do next.

Before THE CHALLENGE, I was one of those people who seemed to have everything—family, career, friends, house—all the 'stuff' you're supposed to want and have. There wasn't a problem with any of them; I loved them all. I really had no idea what I was capable of or what was inside of me, but I did know I was missing something BIG.

For several years now, Wm. James Long has been our family advisor and my mentor, and his wisdom has guided me through both joyful and difficult times. I have always had faith, but never really put it into action. Thankfully, through his focused guidance and the many life lessons learned through THE CHALLENGE, I have since discovered 'myself' by putting my faith to work. I now have a clearer mission and purpose in my life, and renewed faith and confidence that I will accomplish it. I have a sense of security that I never knew was possible and, most importantly, I have found a new inner peace and strength that comforts me in this world of fear, turmoil and uncertainty. It is these qualities which have brought me happiness—not anyone or anything.

And it was all within me, through my choice and my will.

Go forth, Dear Reader, and prepare yourself for THE CHALLENGE of a lifetime.

Lea

Lea Toomcy

SECTION ONE

Improving Your Personal Effectiveness

I

THE FIRST STEP

"The Decision That Changed My Life"

Dear Jack:

I trust my letter finds you well and prospering. I always enjoy writing to you as it gives us time to examine our lives—how they work and what we can do to make them better. In your last letter, you mentioned that you feel it is time for you to grow stronger, examine a few areas that are creating some frustration and avoid decisions that would weaken you. I would be more than happy to share with you my experiences in working to improve my personal effectiveness as well as some time-tested principles that have been of great value to me for building strength.

I recognize that you have already looked carefully at what you want from your life and I know that you have enjoyed measurable success. I see this as an excellent time to get our eyes off of all of the turbulence in the world and focus on ourselves and those we love. I feel it is time to take a close look at how we can take control of our situations and what we can do to find peace and security. So, I look forward to focusing together on this important area in our lives.

We have been friends for a long time and during our friendship we have talked about life as we have seen it in each cycle. I remember when we talked about being able to rely on our education and our careers to provide us with the tools to build ourselves the good life. Remember when we first started to attend the seminars on how to discover ourselves, and how we could rely on subjects such as effective communications and positive mental attitude to get the clarity and strength we sought? I also remember when we attended a workshop on how to build super personal relationships so we could rely on our partners to meet our needs. What an experience that was!

1

When I look back on when I decided to find the answer through seeking who God was, I remember how I struggled to even grasp what had been written about Him and why I should rely on what I had learned.

Do you remember a story I told you several years ago regarding the first time I decided I would seriously examine my life? It was actually while I was watching a football game when it struck me that my mind and my heart were full of turmoil and doubt. I remember looking through a book lying next to the sofa I had been sitting on and discovering a statement that really caught my attention. In it, the author said that we are all controlled by the power of our subconscious mind. He stated that our subconscious runs us like a robot and that it overrides our intellect the vast majority of the time. He then stated that it can control our decisions.

Here I was, enjoying a Super Bowl game while socializing with old friends and suddenly recognizing that I simply was not where I wanted to be in my life. I wasn't happy with what I was experiencing in either my personal or business life, and I knew I needed to do something about it. I remember laying the book down and attempting to have a conversation with my host about the game, realizing that what I really wanted to do was to pick the book back up and read more about what the author had to say.

When I again returned to the page that had grabbed my attention, I was drawn to another paragraph and, although I have no conscious idea today what I had read, I do know that I made a decision. Right in the middle of the third period of that Super Bowl game, I made perhaps one of the most important decisions of my life. My decision was to stop looking at what I didn't want in both my personal and business life, and get my eyes on what I wanted.

You might think that I was just having one of those New Year resolution moments, or that I was caught up in the excitement of the game—but that was not true. I had arrived at that point in my life when I knew it was time for me to decide what my future would be. I can tell you now that it was by the grace of God that I even attended the party let alone opened the book. I could have easily remained at home that day to work, but I went and I found what I needed to start me down a path that would forever change my life.

The following day, I sat down with a note pad and listed ten goals I wanted to achieve. I remember that there were exactly ten goals on my list and I also remember that they were divided between my personal life and business activities. What is interesting is that I now only remember what two of those goals were. One goal was knowledge and the second was wisdom. The reason I don't remember the other eight goals is that one night while focusing on them, all of a sudden, the other eight goals were no longer important. In one single moment in my life I had taken the next step and decided what my most important needs were.

This decision opened the door to the greatest challenge I have ever had. I would have to find the knowledge and wisdom and, more importantly, determine whose knowledge and whose wisdom I could rely on as absolute truth. Although it took me several months to discover the reality of this challenge, I can truthfully tell you that it was one of the most frustrating times of my life. I had no idea how difficult it would be to find the truth, because my subconscious mind would work to undermine my focus. My belief system, my emotions and my intellect kept getting in the way of my seeing the truth and accepting it.

I wanted to bring this experience to your attention because it is important to understand that when we decide that we are ready to open our eyes and ears to new information, we are immediately faced with the dilemma of whether to believe it. We may ask ourselves if we can trust this information to be true. We must examine if we can place our complete confidence in the information, and if there is evidence that the information is wise and strengthening.

I am going to write you a letter every few weeks and share with you a number of principles I have learned that we can rely on. We can work together to apply each principle to every situation you find yourself dealing with, and see how they begin to improve. I know if you invest enough time on each one of your challenges, you will be able to apply the principles, and eliminate the frustration from your life. I hope you will find some of the experiences helpful. It is interesting to see what happens when the principles are not applied. My goal is that you and I will emerge from our examination of these principles and experiences with a greater level of confidence and trust in who and what we can rely on.

I hope that you will also write to me, share your thoughts and feelings, and keep me informed as to how you and your family are doing. I want you to have the very best in your life, and to find the peace and security so many are looking for. Until I write again, take good care of yourself and be at peace.

Your friend always,

James

II

Is There Life After Death?

*"Three Important Principles to Improve
Our Decision-Making"*

Dear Jack:

I trust my letter finds you well and prospering. You have been in my thoughts since my last letter and I have been wondering how you are progressing with your goal to eliminate those issues that have recently presented you with some frustration. Our life experience is the result of many decisions we make and, of course, our participation in other people's decisions. So, I find that any present frustrations can be eliminated by discovering the cause of the frustrations, determining the principles to apply, and taking the action steps to eliminate them.

I have given a great deal of thought to your goal to improve your ability to make decisions. A number of years ago I arrived at a point where I was dead and having a difficult time making new decisions. I was not physically dead but I was financially and emotionally dead. I had also experienced a series of events that took me from having millions of dollars of net worth to almost nothing. I had experienced making the wrong decisions at the wrong time. I had also experienced selling when I should have been buying, and buying when I should have been waiting and building cash reserves.

I don't have the time in this letter to even scratch the surface of all the principles I violated. I certainly didn't set out to hurt myself or my family nor did I intend to hurt anyone else. However, the principles that I violated finally caught up with me and resulted in a slow and painful financial death.

I believe you will benefit from my story about how easy it is to get into financial trouble when investing in real estate. The whole idea behind investing in real estate is to buy properties, rent them out to tenants to cover our expenses, and sit back and watch the property appreciate in value so we can enjoy rental income and then eventually sell the properties at a profit.

When developing real estate, the investment goal is to buy the land, build something on it and sell the developed property to someone for a profit. I began buying investment properties one at a time and then started developing and owning office buildings. In time, I had built a portfolio of a dozen properties which I then used as collateral to borrow money to build housing subdivisions and a couple of apartment complexes. I also bought several parcels of land to subdivide and sell to enable me to build more office buildings, houses and apartments.

Life was good, the economy was good and everything worked well for several years. Of course, I had a number of mortgages and property taxes to pay on each project. There were always a number of additional operating expenses and unexpected surprises. Almost over night, the economy slowed down and I found myself with too many projects and not enough cash. I could have survived financially if I could have maintained an 80% occupancy rate on each building and if expenses on new projects would have remained within my initial budgets. Then, along came a period of high interest rates, a greater number of vacancies and accelerating building costs, and all of a sudden, I was running a little short on cash each month. Actually, I began running between $100,000 to $200,000 short each month and of course much of my money was in the real estate projects. The result was that I had limited cash to cover these deficits. I really can't blame anyone but myself for failing to avoid the challenges but it only took a year or so and I was, financially speaking, terminally ill.

I had forgotten a key rule of real estate investment: The more real estate we own, the more cash reserves we need to provide liquidity in the event of challenging times. I had yet to experience that we cannot always count on our friendly banks to cover our cash needs. In addition, I had overlooked the reality that we cannot count on people to always rent our property nor can we count on projects always being completed as planned. Experience has taught me to always add several "worse case" factors to projected income and expenses as well as to have an extra 10% to 20% of the total amount of cash you project that the project will need. Looking back, I realize that I simply made a number of poor decisions.

During the year following my financial demise, I had numerous discussions with people who had experienced similar challenges. I remember one person asking me what I was going to do and if I wanted strength and peace in my life. Strength and peace—two words I had not considered before. I knew it would require discovering new knowledge and wisdom I did not currently have. This also raised the question of how I could achieve that peace and strength for I suddenly realized how important they were to me. I must tell you that seeking peace and strength is not an easy task. I am forever thankful that I refused to settle for the standard answers I heard from a number of self-appointed teachers and prophets. I am also thankful that I did not get lost in what I knew or what my level of understanding of life was at that point in my life.

Although I had been raised as a child in a minister's home, I realized that I knew little, if anything, about God's principles. In college, I minored in psychology and had attended numerous conferences over the years on the human mind. As a businessman, I had also participated in several leadership and personal growth programs. However, when faced with this devastating financial crisis, I realized I had learned few fundamentals I could apply to my present situation. I also felt the vast majority of these programs hadn't and couldn't provide me with the kind of clarity and strength I was seeking.

Some people I talked with told me that the answer was in continuing education and that I would be wise to return and strengthen myself through continued study. And, there were others who pointed out that I had been too aggressive in my investments and should take the safe path and let other people handle my investments.

My journey to obtain knowledge and wisdom had lasted about four months when I met Peter, a bright, personable fellow who happened to be in the advertising business. We begin meeting for lunch to talk about common interests and our dreams and goals for the future. Peter was not what you would label a religious person, nor had he achieved any measure of success in either his financial or business life. But Peter was wise enough to give me the first clue I needed to take the first step to get the needed knowledge I sought. You ask what was his clue?

One day, Peter asked me a very important question. His question was, did I know what I wanted from my life? He knew I had learned a lot from helping others to organize and manage their businesses and that I had achieved some past success. But his question really got my attention.

You may ask why was his question so important and why would it provide me with a major principle? The reason was that Peter opened my eyes to a very important issue. It struck me then that if I knew clearly what I wanted from my life, I would have taken the first step toward finding the specific knowledge and wisdom I sought.

Had I not already asked to receive knowledge and wisdom? Had I not already asked to achieve strength? Was I not seeking peace in my life? Was I not ready and willing to take action in my personal and business life only after making sure that my actions were based on the right decisions? Yes, I had focused on all of these issues, but I had not taken the time to determine clearly my purpose.

I told Peter I had not yet decided what my future would look like. I then asked him if he knew where I could go to get the knowledge necessary to prepare myself. Peter listened and suggested that I meet with a friend of his who was working as a business coach. He told me that his friend John had helped him look at life differently and felt I would benefit from meeting him.

The next day, I called John to arrange a time we could meet. When I hung up I realized how excited I was just thinking about the possibility of establishing a new life for myself. This was the first time in several months that I felt like things were going to be okay. I was literally starting over and I felt it might be a tough journey because the economy at that time was not conducive for new growth. I also lacked the capital to seed my recovery. All I had was a burning desire to be reborn and to achieve something in my new life that would bring me renewed happiness as well as some quality of life for my family.

I will never forget the day I met John for the first time. We were sitting in an office so small that one would quickly realize that John was certainly not attempting to put on any financial airs. As a matter of fact, we were meeting in his wife's chiropractic office and I don't believe he even had an office of his own. This didn't matter. I was there to seek truth and wisdom and he knew it. He asked me if I was clear about what I wanted to achieve during our work together. My answer was that I was tired of the cycles I'd experienced in the past and wanted strength. I told him that I wanted to eliminate anything in me or around me that would create weakness.

John then asked me if I was ready to choose highest purpose for my life and was I ready to find what that was for me. He told me that highest purpose strengthens and is a core issue when making all of one's decisions. I told him that I knew he had discovered an important principle and that I was ready to choose highest purpose. John asked me to simply choose it and speak my decision. Neither of us tried to define what highest purpose meant that day but I knew that this was something much more than any one's intellectual or emotional viewpoint.

What I have learned since the day I made my decision is that purpose strengthens. I know that we can determine what highest purpose is prior to making any important decisions in either our personal, business or financial life. John had not tried to preach me a sermon nor had he attempted to convert me to any religion. He simply gave me a principle that I knew was important. I felt that highest purpose was from God but I had already figured out that a lot of people have a different picture of who God is and what He expects from us. Let's face it, millions of people have been killed arguing over who knows God and what His purpose is for us. However, I realized that highest purpose is God's purpose and therefore I wanted to examine more about Him and His ways.

John then asked me if I was ready to become a person of highest truth. He said that truth strengthens and that anything that is not true weakens us. He said that we all know people who have the tendency to lie frequently and how no one really enjoys these people because we cannot count on their words or their agreements. He also said that people draw conclusions before taking the time to determine if they are in highest truth. I also knew that truth is often clouded by our feelings and emotions in the moment. Again, I knew immediately that truth does strengthen and that I wanted to become a person of highest truth. At that moment in time, I chose to seek highest truth before making any decision or any agreement.

The last question John asked me was on the surface simple but more difficult for me to understand than the first two questions. He asked me if I was ready to establish all of my relationships in highest love. I suspect that when many people think about the subject of love they may get love confused with feelings of romantic and even sexual love. But, I knew one thing and that was love was good for us and that love could withstand all of life's most difficult challenges. So, I agreed that this was an important principle for accepting self and establishing solid relationships. I told him that I chose to be in highest love from that point forward.

What I have learned about love since I made the choice to be in highest love is that it can manifest great peace. I've also learned the opposite of peace is turmoil and, left with which one I prefer, I always want peace. I am very happy that I made up my mind that day with John to choose to develop all of my relationships in highest love and simply avoid people who always seem to be in turmoil.

From that one visit with John, I received a marvelous gift. The gift was a new-found awareness of the principles I needed as the foundation for living my life and making all of my decisions. This has given me confidence that if my decisions are to yield strong and predictable results then they must always be in highest purpose, truth and love.

I want you to know that I value our relationship. I also want you to know how much I want you to enjoy life and be free of anything that would create turmoil. I hope these three principles will be as helpful to you as they have been to me. Everything begins with choice and from that point forward, we are able to find our way as we apply each principle. These principles I have shared with you can support us in rebuilding our lives from any challenging experience.

I must go now but will write again soon. Until then, I trust you will enjoy peace and joy in everything you do.

Your friend always,

James

III

HOW IMPORTANT IS STRENGTH IN OUR LIVES?

"Strength is a Prerequisite for Power"

Dear Jack:

I trust my letter finds you well and prospering. I am happy you enjoyed learning about the principles that I learned from John. Many of the people I have shared them with have told me how powerful they are as they have worked to create a new future and develop solid relationships. What I want to examine in this letter is to address your question concerning how to build strength.

Strength is the opposite of weakness and is a prerequisite for our growth and survival. Strength will develop over time as we eliminate weakness, build strong thinking and decision-making habits, and modify our attitudes. It doesn't come easy nor can it be given to us by politicians or parents. Strength is one of the foundational requirements if we want to be an independent person and achieve a level of true security in our lives.

When we stop to think about life and its realities, we discover that we are not born strong but come into life totally dependent. Our educational system lacks courses on strength-building or decision-making, so we do not learn early in our life how to become strong. Companies often stress the importance of becoming strong as well as becoming good decision-makers. But often, the people at the top end up making the decisions. So we often fail to be able to build and demonstrate strength in our companies.

In my last letter to you, I shared the principles that control our decision-making. There are three factors involved as we begin focusing on building strength. Before we review them, we should first examine the following question. How can we begin to rebuild ourselves from our failures and our negative financial and business experiences? Maybe the solution lies in science or maybe it lies in our spiritual teachings. What if both teachings are saying the same thing? What if we have had the answers for centuries and simply failed to see them clearly?

How do you make your decisions? Most of us take several steps depending on who we see as our authority figures and our decision-making habits. Some of us want to be sure that we have assurances and guarantees before we make any decision. Others rely on who else is doing the same thing they are considering doing.

Some people focus on what is best for them in the moment, while others make most of their decisions based on how the decision will affect their personal or business partners. Needless to say, our customary approach to decision-making depends on a number of factors including our image of self and our emotions concerning each subject which requires our decision.

I have discovered that the first step to build strength is to base all of our decisions on the three primary principles which I have already introduced to you. Again, these principles are: (1) Purpose strengthens; (2) Truth strengthens; and (3) Love strengthens.

Before we make any decision, we can examine what it is we are attempting to achieve and then apply these principles as we evaluate our options and what we want to achieve. When applying these principles for making our financial decisions, we should also tie them to basic business principles to enhance the probability of our financial success. In addition, adding the principle of knowing clearly what we want to achieve is an important element toward building strength.

Before I go any further, I want to answer a question you might have already asked yourself. That question is, what in the world do I mean when I state that love strengthens? What does this have to do with making wise financial decisions? Surprisingly enough, this principle may be affecting you far more than you realize. Some people make their financial decisions from emotional weaknesses, from a fear of not being loved, and from feelings that the things they want to buy will make them more accepted at home and in their community.

Several clients I have talked with have admitted that they have spent money on their children that they should have saved for other financial goals because they felt guilty about divorces or for working so many long hours. Others overspend because they simply can't say no to their children's requests.

Love is not what we have been sold on television and in the movies. Love is based on acceptance of self and others that grounds the relationship in peace, trust, and in meeting each other's needs. Therefore, financial decisions that do not meet our real needs create turmoil in our relationships and may lead to antagonism and anger. These emotions can lead to resentment and guilt and sometimes lead to hostility. When this happens, people then may set out to get even for what they perceive has happened to them. Don't forget that one of the major causes for divorce is over the issue of money. So, decisions that are made without taking into consideration our relationships with others can lead to challenges which, if not addressed, can easily kill us financially. They can also kill the relationship.

What about the subject of truth. How do we know what is true? We hear so much on television about who is right and who is wrong. We hear various opinions on literally hundreds of topics such as how to invest our money as well as what to buy and what to sell. Are you sure you know what the truth is regarding who to form friendships with and who to do business with? You see, discovering truth is not easy. But, truth does assist us in building strength as well as strong relationships.

Now I want to introduce another valuable principle for building strength. This principle stems from the most basic elements which ensure our very existence will continue. The principle affirms that in order for a thought to be manifest in the physical, we must have a clear picture of what it will look like. In other words, we must visualize clearly exactly what we want to achieve.

I heard a true story several years ago about the experience of one of the pilots while he was in a Viet Nam prisoner of war camp. To keep his sanity, this man played 18 holes of golf every day. He would visualize every shot he would make as he played each hole in his mind. He would etch into his mind every stroke and every swing as he selected and utilized each golf club in his bag. Day after day, week after week, he played golf in his mind. Every day, his goal was to shoot par on each course he played.

As the story goes, this pilot was eventually released and returned to the United States. Shortly after his return he was invited to play in a golf tournament. He had played virtually no actual games of golf for over two years but on that day, his score was a perfect par on a very difficult course. Here we see a great example of the power of visualization. We must see clearly what we want to achieve and keep that picture etched in our mind every day until our goal is manifest.

I have introduced these principles to you for a reason. The reason is that if there is to be life after financial death, we must eliminate the causes that could lead to your financial or business demise, and replace them with decisions and actions that will lead to sound financial and business health. If we want to become financially successful and reach the point in life where we are financially free, then we will have to become strong. We will want to apply each principle daily because there are too many people and too many temptations that can get us off track and lead us back into a life of financial weakness and eventual death.

We must become wise decision-makers and always remember that life is full of decisions. One poor decision never kills us, rather it's always a series of decisions that do us in.

In my next letter, I will share my discoveries on how the way we see things and our feelings and emotions can weaken us. I must go now and prepare for a trip to St. Thomas. We are having our house painted with several new colors so we may be in for a real surprise when we return. I hope you are enjoying life and look forward to our next visit.

Your friend always,

James

IV

DOES THE WAY WE SEE THINGS CONTROL THE WAY WE TRY TO MANAGE THEM?

"We Cannot Solve Challenges with the Same Thinking That Created Them"

Dear Jack:

I've finally found a few moments to write to you again. I trust my letter finds you and your family well and enjoying life. We are all busy expanding our transition planning services to be able to assist the people who are now being asked to take early retirement. This is requiring many people in our community to rethink their future.

I mentioned in my last letter that I would share some of my discoveries about how our belief system can weaken and limit the way we see things. The discoveries you shared in your last letter were very thought-provoking. Yes, I do know that the way we see things controls the way we try to manage them. I have been thinking about times in the past when we suddenly discover that we were seeing certain things in our life differently and we then began to see new options or new solutions. I am experiencing several changes in my life lately and I decided that instead of dealing with the stress of moving into the unknown that I would relax and pay more attention to what was happening to me. What I am discovering is that my views of certain situations are changing and as my views change, I am managing each situation differently.

Have you ever had this experience? I have been looking around my community to see what people's attitudes are about current world events and I have discovered, as usual, that each person sees these events differently.

15

What is consistent in their thinking is that many have become more alarmed about each situation and few have identified any solutions. I believe that no matter how we view any challenge the first step in solving it is to first identify what the challenge actually is.

I have a growing suspicion that our national and international challenges will not be solved by anyone's current thinking. My conclusion is that we are wise to focus on our own issues and plans and build our own trust, faith and confidence in our plans for the future.

As I have focused on my own plans for the future, I have had to ask myself some hard questions. I have also had to examine where I have any feelings of insecurity and where I may lack total confidence. I have found that it has been very beneficial to step back and challenge myself to see if I can look at each situation differently and more importantly, discover how I can approach each issue differently. While taking these steps, I have made some new discoveries and also found several new solutions. All in all, I found it to be a great experience once I was willing to take the necessary steps. I want to share some of my new discoveries with you.

I have discovered that our vision is often clouded by subconscious feelings and emotions. We don't always see issues as they actually exist or make sound decisions due to these feelings and emotions. Also, the feeling that something is better than nothing has blocked so many from improving their situation, and building confidence and security. This is true regardless of what area of our lives we are focused on.

To understand my first discovery requires that you go through an actual exercise. Would you be willing to list all of the issues in your life you would like to change to feel more confident and secure about your future, and then take the time to determine if you honestly see them as they really are? You will be surprised at the outcome as you step back and look at each issue to examine how you can see it differently.

In this letter, I want to share with you my experience with two of my clients, Grace and Gordon, and how they placed themselves in positions of doubt and fear. I will share with you how their fear led to challenges in money management and challenges in their personal relationships. So, turn off your television and I will share with you a peek into the lives of Grace and Gordon for a while.

I bet you know someone who is always telling you how much he or she wants or needs to change something in their lives but is never willing to do anything about it. Many times people fail to take action because they have a deep-seated feeling or emotion blocking their ability to focus on a solution. In Grace's case, her unhappiness was the result of a meaningless job and a weak personal relationship. I've known Grace for more than seven years and see her every year during tax season. Every time we got together in the past, Grace complained about her job and how much she wished she worked somewhere else. If I had let her go on and on about each subject she was unhappy about, we could have had a "pity party" lasting all afternoon. Grace felt sorry for herself and further felt that she was stifled in her present job. It didn't take very long to get the message that she hated it. Do you know anyone who is in Grace's situation?

For several years, when Grace would remind me of her unhappiness, I would ask her what type of job she wanted and what she was willing to do to find a new one. Every time I asked, she would repeat to me that she did not like the person she reported to and if only the company would replace that person, maybe things would get better. I could never get Grace to look past her problem, so after a while, I quit trying and simply acknowledged that she was unhappy and hoped things would improve for her.

It was not until last fall that I finally got Grace's attention. What happened was that her company began laying off people in her department and she became concerned that she would also lose her job. Now we need to add to her unrest the other issue that Grace frequently brought up when she talked about her unhappiness and concern about her future. This issue was that she and her husband had argued about their finances for years. She told me that they both had substantial disagreement about the whole subject of their finances as well as each person's strategies for managing it. Her husband had taken over paying the bills four or five years ago and made sure that all of Grace's income went directly toward paying their bills.

Grace not only hated her job, she seldom got to enjoy any portion of her income as it all went toward payment of their debts. As you might expect, when I asked her if she would be interested in meeting with one of my associates to help her and her husband with some cash-flow planning, she reminded me that her husband handled the bills and doubted he was in the mood to let anyone else know about their financial challenges.

One day, Grace called me to ask what I thought about borrowing $35,000 from her 401k so that her husband could pay off several accounts that were causing her some anxiety. Her concern was that she might be one of the next people to be laid off by her company and if that happened, she would have to pay taxes on this loan, as she would not be able to repay the loan. It was during that phone conversation that I finally got her attention. I said to her, "It sounds to me that you will be out of a job within a few weeks. It appears that this is inevitable."

I certainly didn't know if the company would terminate Grace or whether she would even hear what I said, but I felt it was a good time to see if I could get her attention. For the first time, Grace said to me, "I guess I better start preparing to find a different job." For the first time in years, Grace had shifted her focus from the problem to the solution. As Grace discovered for herself, one cannot take the steps to solve a problem until one is ready to focus on solving it.

We all have an area in our life we wish to change or eliminate. There is absolutely no one on this earth today who does not have something in his or her life that needs to be dealt with, in order to gain greater strength and peace in their life. We are either in a state of peace or in a state of turmoil. We cannot experience feelings of absolute peace if we have something that is creating turmoil in our life. Just as physical death is an absolute experience, so is absolute peace, and total peace can exist only as we achieve absolute confidence in ourselves and in our future and learn how to take action, free of weakening feelings and emotions.

Since the fear of the unknown can block us from taking the steps necessary to achieve change in our lives, many of us won't let go of the jobs and people that have weakened us. We hold on because we are afraid of what we will experience from the next job or the next relationship. The way we see these issues controls our ability to change. We often put up with something because we believe it is better than nothing. However, I have found that you can't have what you want until you free yourself of what you don't want. Have you ever found yourself in that situation? This is a valuable principle to remember and apply whenever necessary.

Take a few minutes and ask yourself what you should do with any fears you may have about anything. Then see if you can identify what you are holding on to that may be blocking you from conquering these fears. See if you can identify what is blocking you from changing each situation. Remember that for things to change, we must choose to change. We cannot change another person or a company. We can only achieve change in ourselves and this change can begin when we begin focusing on what we want.

Getting back to my phone conversation with Grace, she then made an interesting statement. She said, "I am afraid that if I leave my present employer, my department will be in real trouble as I'm the only one there who is holding things together." Out spilled the core reason she had stayed in a job that she really did not like. The reason was that she felt important in her position and, worse yet, responsible for the welfare of her department. Her emotional center was on how important this job made her feel. When I thought about her situation, I wondered how anyone could place their emotional center on a job they hated. Fortunately, her fear of losing her income became stronger than her emotional center and her fear of moving on to a new company. The way she saw her situations had weakened her.

It has now been about eight months from the day Grace shifted her attention from her unhappiness and her weakening point of view to the reality that it was better for her to move forward and take action. I believe it was her fear of being without an income that finally overrode her other emotions regarding her relationship with her job.

Grace finally took her first step and began determining what job and what environment would meet her needs and best utilize her skills and talents. She then took the second step by talking with several women at her church about her decision to find a new job and what type of job she was interested in. Within two weeks she was invited by one of these women to meet with the woman's husband, who had formed a new company and needed an office manager to oversee customer services. Three weeks later she resigned from her old job and is now, for the first time in years, enjoying her new position as the new office manager in the new company.

There is another side to Grace's story I want to tell you about. This side of the story is yet to be completed, but has taken on a new direction that can only lead to improvement in Grace's life. When Grace accepted her new position with the new company, she actually agreed to a reduction in pay during the first two years of employment. She made this agreement willingly so she could participate in future profits. This decision created quite a bit of discussion between her and her husband about their financial situation and her involvement in their budget planning. He was quite upset over her willingness to take a reduction in salary, and basically held her responsible for their financial challenges.

During one of their ongoing discussions about their finances, Grace finally raised the possibility that their spending was the problem, and maybe they should take a close look at why they always seemed to be spending more than they earn. Grace told me later that they both concluded that they were spending too much on entertainment and travel, in an attempt to escape their general unhappiness. Her husband admitted he had not felt good about their relationship for quite some time. He had compensated through socializing with other couples who had greater resources to pay for the various dinners and trips.

Today, Grace and her husband are currently reassessing every area of their relationship, and are taking equal responsibility for their present financial situation. This will lead to a better future for both of them regardless of what direction they take.

I was going to tell you also about Gordon in this letter but must close now to prepare for a meeting. I want you to take care of yourself and get more exercise. I will write again soon and tell you about Gordon.

Your friend always,

James

V

ARE WE CONTROLLED BY OUR PAST?

"Principles to Create a New Future"

Dear Jack:

I trust my letter finds you well and prospering. I enjoyed your recent letter and agree with you that sometimes we don't know why we feel the way we do or, for that matter, why we worry about issues we shouldn't worry about. Considering how much of our feelings are hidden deep in our subconscious mind, it is interesting to consider how much we are controlled by our past.

Thinking about the past reminds me of a recent trip my wife Marcelle and I took to England. On the third day of this voyage to explore England and its history, I was awakened at 6:00 AM and asked if I wanted to go visit Bath. I'm talking about Bath, England. The color brochure pictured Bath as a beautiful city initially built by the Romans and later expanded as the English aristocrats discovered the healing power of its underground springs. Everywhere we had gone, we had seen monuments of the past. There were buildings that had been built 300 years ago and evidence of its culture as far back as 1,000 years ago. So, I agreed that Bath would be our destination that day knowing it would be another day I would spend both looking at and thinking about the past.

As we toured the countryside around Bath, we discovered Lacock, a small medieval village consisting of an abbey and about sixty row houses. Walking through Lacock was like taking a trip back in time. What an experience to realize that people had lived there for perhaps a thousand years. I imagine this little village had an interesting past. It showed its physical age in a unique and charming way. I am certain the walls of its old houses still hold thousands of secrets that will never be told to anyone but they remain there etched in the stones like grooves in a record.

Each of us have stored in our mind all of the events of our past. In our subconscious mind is hidden the memory of thousands of experiences.

These experiences become the foundation for our image of self and how we deal with our lives. Our successes and failures are all hidden in our mind and automatically guide us as we deal with each new situation we are confronted with. I want you to stop reading for just one moment and think about this reality. Then, understand that you can take control of your subconscious through conscious and creative choice. It will help you begin to take control over those memories—memories that serve to weaken you and block you from becoming more confident and secure.

Social psychologists tell us that we are operating from our subconscious mind over 90% of the time which results in automatic behavior. They say this behavior controls us through what we believe to be true and our conditioned responses. If this is so, then our feelings about our ability to handle any important area in our lives control how we see each dimension of the situation. Simply stated, if we believe something is true, then we proceed to take action, or no action, based on this subconscious belief. These hidden feelings control how we feel about ourselves as parents, how we feel about our current financial situation, and of course how we feel about both our personal and business relationships.

We are often controlled by our feelings and emotions that are highly edited by our emotional barometer. As an example, if you want to understand the root issues between many people in the Arab world and American society, you need to go back to the times of Abraham and his two sons, Ishmael and Isaac. When you realize that the current turmoil between these two blood lines began some 4,000 years ago, then you can begin to see there are deep-seeded feelings locked into individuals' subconscious that color how they see their situation.

Maybe sometime in the future we can talk about the turmoil between these two blood lines of Abraham. I only use it as an example of how our subconscious mind controls both individuals as well as groups of individuals. My point is that we are controlled by those beliefs and fears we do not consciously know we have which can magnify our feelings of frustration and concern, as we look at any present challenges.

On our trip to England, we also visited Windsor Palace, the country home of the Queen of England. If you have not yet visited Windsor, you would be amazed at its grandeur which overpowers the countryside surrounding it. I have taken you to Windsor to see something else about the past, for within the walls of Windsor Palace lie room after room that have been occupied over the years by different members of the royal family.

Even today, they are occupied by one or another of the current royal family members, most of whom are struggling with their past and their life challenges, even with their wealth and stature. Every one of its current occupants is also in a transition, and neither money nor title will protect them from having to deal with what is in their subconscious mind. Our past affects our present transition regardless of who we are or how much money or fame we have attained.

In your last letter you mentioned that you are currently going through a transition in your life. I have been around many people during their transitions. Sometimes I feel that we are all in transition in one way or another. People may be just married or just divorced or they may be starting a new job or ending one. Many times they come to me when they are preparing to start a new business while other times, they come when the business is lying in ruin. One thing I have learned about transition is that it can bring out fears in each of us. Here again we can see how our lives are affected by fear of the unknown.

In looking back at how a number of different people have handled their transitions, I think about Michelle. Let me tell you something up front: Some of those I talked with had no idea what was going to happen to them when they first realized that they were being driven in a new direction. I use the term "driven" because their motivation to go in a new direction was certainly not based on an intellectual decision. It was coming from their feelings and emotions. I could hear it in their attitudes and feel it in their words every time they spoke about their situation.

Let's start with Michelle and how she came to our offices. I first learned about Michelle from my old friend Mark. Mark called one day to tell me that he had met a woman at his church who was having great difficulty with her marriage and needed some financial planning as it looked like she and her husband would be ending their marriage within a month or two. I invited Mark to bring her in to see me and told him he was welcome to join us if she would be more comfortable with him there.

When I met Michelle, I saw someone struggling with her transition. She was having a tough time dealing with the reality of her situation although I can only remember one reasonably smooth divorce in my entire life. Her key issue was letting go of her belief that her husband should have a greater level of financial responsibility to her and the children after twenty years of marriage. She simply could not let go of her belief that she could change his mind about leaving the family, and she was certain that their pastor could help her husband through his midlife crisis and anger.

We spent almost the entire first meeting listening to her stories about Joe's verbal and physical abuse. Michelle was a real talker, and talked on and on about her situation. Each time I would ask her to tell me how she wanted to proceed to increase her income, she would begin talking again about Joe, how confused he appeared to be and how badly he treated her. She was blocking her ability to get through her transition by feelings about the past. She had not accepted the reality that what she had received in the past from that relationship was no longer true.

I asked her what her financial situation would be if they divorced and if she could survive financially. She told me that during the eight months they had already been separated, that Joe had reduced her support payments twice and that she would not be able to survive financially without increasing her income by $2,000 per month.

During the last ten minutes of our first meeting, I asked Michelle if she was willing to face the future alone. I could have given her hope or simply let it be okay for her to stay focused on the past, but I let the words come out because I wanted her to be able to move forward with her life. As you would expect, my words brought up tears and some anger she had been holding onto for months and months. Out came the sorrow and frustration. Out came the hurt and fear of being alone. We sat there for about four or five minutes while she had a good cry.

She took the first step forward that day by dealing with her anger. It was her anger at herself for allowing this situation to reach its then present condition that was immobilizing Michelle. In a very short time Michelle became calm and ready to continue our conversation. I then asked her if she would agree to complete an assignment. Her assignment would be to write Joe a letter and let him know that he was free to go his own way and that she would not attempt to hold him back in any manner.

Although she again reminded Mark and me how hurt she was over his recent behavior, she agreed to write the letter. Her major concern was why Joe had refused to take financial responsibility for their five children. She couldn't understand why he was behaving so badly. As we ended our first meeting, I realized that Michelle was struggling with her past and had little faith in her future.

After several conversations with one of our transition planners and the development of an action plan, Michelle has now weathered eight more months of separation and recently introduced me to her new male companion who she met at her church's singles group. She is going to school and has taken a position as an assistant administrator of a day school. Although she is still feeling the effects of the emotional toll of the divorce, she is well on her way through the healing process and has a much brighter view of her future. Her days of personal torture are over, and her nights of wondering what went wrong in her marriage are past. What helped her was her decision to move forward and concentrate on her future.

Our mind is a magnificent organ. We can view it as a palace filled with rooms, each holding memories of the past, while having the capacity to welcome new memories and new images of who we are and what we can become. We can create a completely new interior through conscious creative choice, or we can continue to live with the old décor forever. It is all in our hands or, better stated, all in our ability to paint over the old wall colors with new colors. We can replace the old wallpaper patterns with new ones, and we can toss out the outdated furniture and replace it with new furniture. It all starts with choice.

For each of us to successfully move through any of our life transitions, we must have faith in our ability to reach our new destination. The opposite emotion from faith is fear. Fear immobilizes us, while faith empowers us. So, you ask me, how do you replace fear with faith? The first step is to let go of fear and focus on what you want to achieve in the future. Faith is an important principle to apply as we refocus from what we don't want to what we want.

I hope you will focus on your future and identify specific goals. Just reach down deep in your heart and find that place where you have hidden away your dreams. None of us is born to fail nor are we born to bear the burdens of others. We also were not born to be another person's slave, or to be their whipping post. We were born to learn and apply God's laws so that we will be fruitful and abundant. Although it will take time and effort, we can eliminate fear and overcome past feelings and emotions.

I must close this letter as I want to take a good long walk and focus on the changes that are happening in my life. It is very exciting to see changes unfolding and to know that I have had a part in bringing forth what I have asked for. Until I write again, I wish you the best and trust you will enjoy peace and abundance in every area of your life.

Your friend always,

James

VI

CAN WE QUIT REACTING AND BECOME A PERSON OF ACTION?

"Principles for Developing Faith and Overcoming Anger"

Dear Jack:

I really enjoyed your last letter and understand how you feel regarding the fears that arise when focusing on new dreams and goals. I also realize how much you have counted on your present career meeting your long-term needs and that you are angry at what is now happening in your company. I have found that the best way to manage fear is to have faith, and the best way to manage anger is to focus on what we are willing to do to change our situation. I also realize this will always require that we take action but before we move forward, we will want to examine exactly what we need to do to quit reacting.

When I look at the subject of faith, I recognize that there are two very important issues to examine. The first issue is who to have faith in. The second issue is how to believe something is going to manifest that, in the moment, does not exist. Many of my friends and clients immediately talk about faith in God when we start talking about the subject. We have literally hundreds if not thousands of religions throughout the world and they all have one thing in common. Do you know what that one thing is? The answer is they all teach faith, while pointing to a higher power that is able to conquer fear. Only through faith can we achieve this objective. Only through faith can we venture into the unknown with confidence that we will achieve our goals.

Each of our life transitions presents an unknown destination that we will often travel to alone. Sometimes we feel all alone as we struggle to move forward and find our path. We often feel like we are in the dark and that there is no one there to guide us. Sometimes we want others to travel with us, only to find that they are either not interested or not willing to go with us. It is very easy to feel lost and sometimes we feel alone.

But you see we are not alone nor are we lost. God's principles are always with us. We are only lost in our feelings and emotions, lost in our anger and fear, lost in our resentment and guilt. We are separated from the peace we can have through faith and confidence in God, in His principles and in ourselves. Yes, it is true that we must have confidence also in ourselves and in our personal and business partners. We cannot simply have confidence in God or in others; we must take the time to develop our own confidence or we cannot take the necessary steps we need to take to handle our own transitions effectively.

The woman I wrote about in my last letter, Michelle, must have found her faith in herself to be able to take a new job that three months earlier she felt she was not qualified to do. She must have had renewed faith in herself to venture into a new relationship. Where did she start her path to finding faith in herself? The answer is that she started down the path by dealing with her anger. Her reactions triggered by her anger toward her husband had been blocking her from moving forward.

So, when faced with fear or doubt, we can apply a very important principle. This principle is that when we ask God for anything that is in highest purpose, truth and love we must expect Him to deliver it. We must expect Him to deliver while we focus on what we have asked for until it arrives. This continuous action builds faith and reinforces our trust in God and His principles. Only then can we move forward free of fear and doubt.

Now, I want to talk about an emotion that produces great reactions. This is the emotion of anger which triggers predictable behavior. The most important thing I can tell you about anger is that it immobilizes us and keeps us from being able to move forward, whenever it is important to move forward in our lives. People often tell me that they feel that anger is good because it forces them to take action. This is a misconception as anger forces us to react, which is an automatic reflex based on old feelings and emotions.

It doesn't matter whether our situation revolves around financial issues, business issues or even personal issues. What matters is that we quit reacting and start choosing new alternatives for ourselves. What matters is that we choose to change our situation and begin with the end in mind. Our "end in mind" is our goal for the future.

The principle to apply to achieve change is to quit reacting and choose to change. Once we have chosen to quit reacting due to our present feelings and emotions, we can choose our new direction. Only then can we begin to develop our new plan for the future. Once we have determined that we can change the situation, we will have taken the first step toward change.

We would also be wise to get our eyes off of all of the economic and political issues we have absolutely no control over. We can only change those areas in our lives we have the capacity to change. Just as we cannot change another person, we certainly cannot change other governments or corporations. We can only change ourselves.

The thing about change is that we often fear it because, regardless of how much we dislike our present situation, it is still something we know about, while the future is unknown. So, it is valuable to apply the principles that will help us through our transitions.

I trust you will review these principles from time to time to see how well you are applying them when you want to improve the management of your finances, your business and your relationships. I hope you will develop faith in these principles and, most importantly, I trust you will apply the principles 100% of the time. It does not do us much good to apply the principles 50% of the time, nor will it help us very much if you only apply them when you have exhausted your own personal strategies.

No matter what our present position is concerning the existence of a Supreme Being, or how we feel about the subject of spiritual strength, we will be able to see strength in the principles and achieve positive action steps if we apply them. When we have personal knowledge that something is true, then we no longer need to evaluate it or worry about it. I encourage you to apply the principles I am sharing with you for you to achieve change in your life.

Talking about fear and anger can be mentally exhausting so I am going to close this letter and get some exercise. I look forward to hearing from you soon. Until we communicate again, I wish you peace and joy.

Your friend always,

James

VII

ARE THERE PRINCIPLES FOR ACHIEVING SUCCESSFUL LIFE TRANSITIONS?

"Discovering Your Personal Mission"

Dear Jack:

I trust my letter finds you well and prospering. I am well and enjoying developing a new regional expansion program which has kept us very busy. I will tell you more about our expansion plans soon. I enjoyed your recent letter and have looked forward to writing you for several days to share a few principles I am confident will support you in your present transition.

When we first face any of our major life transitions, we find that we have arrived at a place in our life where we are being drawn into a rather fascinating web. The reason it is fascinating is that we have known for some time that we were becoming caught up in the situation. We knew in our hearts that we were marching toward it but we have yet to admit to ourselves that we are trapped in it. We have been slowly drawn into this web with thoughts and feelings that slowly bring us to the point where we have concluded that we must do something.

Our natural inclination would be to either run from it or fight it. These two automatic reactions are commonly known as those of "fight" or "flight." If you will watch any dog or cat, you will find that both will automatically take one of these two paths when threatened. We also will follow the same automatic path unless we consciously choose not to. When we run away from any challenge, we have failed to confront it and conquer it. If we try to fight it, without first deciding clearly what we want to accomplish, we will find that all we have done is make it worse. Remember that for every action, there is an equal reaction and when we push people, they will push us back. When we judge others, they will in turn judge us. When looking at this fundamental truth, we find a principle we can count on to be true, and truth strengthens us.

With these thoughts in mind, I ask you to identify which one of God's principles is the one you would apply to take the first step? What has He given all of us that we can use to change any situation? The answer is the power of choice. You have the ability to choose a new direction for yourself, regardless of what you think or how you feel about your present dilemma. The first step to change is to choose to change.

The second principle to apply to achieve change is to determine what you want and what you need. Many people I talk with tell me what they don't want and most will talk on endlessly about their issues. Our newspapers are filled with stories that remind us that there are challenges all around us. Our television news stations bring us reports of financial and political struggles all over the world and then invest hours debating what went wrong or whether we made the wrong decision. We are bombarded with people telling us what they don't want.

Listening to all of this takes a considerable amount of time and energy (and can very well immobilize us). As we worry about all of the various problems around us and our own challenges, we have very little time or energy left to look at new solutions. Unless we stand back from our situation and decide what we want and were we want to go, there is little chance we will get there. After you are finished reading my letter, I encourage you to take a few minutes and begin the process of thinking about what you want now and where you want to go. Do not do anything else about the situation until you have applied this principle and discovered your answers.

Once you have determined what you want, you must prepare yourself to enable you to achieve the highest probability for success. In order to prepare ourselves, we must prepare ourselves on four different levels. You will need to prepare yourself physically, emotionally, intellectually and spiritually. Remember that each one of these levels of preparation takes work. Change will not come without applying this principle and fully taking these steps.

When we take a close look at each level of preparation, we will find that we not only must work on each level but also we cannot work on it without a plan of action. What this means is that our first action plan is not on the mission itself, but on preparing ourselves to take the journey to achieve the mission. This is where so many people make their first mistake. They get excited about their new goal and run off unprepared to achieve it. When they fail, there are driven deeper into despair and right back where they started.

Laying out your plan to prepare yourself may not be an easy task, so I recommend that you obtain help with this area of your planning. As you look at each level you must prepare, you will be able to determine who can best assist you and guide you in each of these levels. Although we are talking about change, I remind you that these principles also apply as we discover that we need to refocus on our mission and discover that we have gotten off course in our journey.

Organizing your plan to prepare yourself will require that you modify your habits and improve your skills. It will require that you also improve your knowledge in the appropriate areas. Most importantly, it will require that you change your attitude about yourself and others. When considering the importance of these four elements, by far the most important one is attitude. Your attitude toward yourself and toward your mission will control your ability to achieve it.

The fourth principle in your journey to achieve your new transition plan is to take conscious creative action. By applying this principle, you are moving forward now in faith toward the future goal. You cannot as yet touch or feel the evidence of your goal, nor do you have any guarantee you will achieve it. However, as already stated, you must have a clear picture of what it will look like when you arrive and confidence you will reach your destination.

Now we begin to see how faith and confidence each play such a large role in transition planning. The greater the level of passion and enthusiasm you have toward the goal, the easier it is to take the steps in the unknown. The greater the level of confidence and faith you have that you will reach the goal, the greater the level of probability that you will reach it.

It's time now to tell you about Roger. Roger will forever stand out in my mind as someone who figured out very rapidly how things work. When I first met Roger, he was operating a small business that was not supporting either him or any of his employees. He had gotten himself into so much debt that he could barely pay his suppliers and hadn't given his three employees a raise in pay for over five years. Business was slow and there was little money to allocate to marketing and sales to develop new customers. It was quite obvious that Roger had lost his faith, and unless things changed, would see his business die within a short time.

It was not that Roger didn't see the challenges, he simply could not decide what to do about them. Otherwise, he had an outstanding mind and was on top of each and every technical issue within his business. When we first met, Roger asked if I would be willing to write a business plan that would tell him what he needed to do to move forward and to correct his situation. He was in the business of custom designing systems to interface in moving information through the Internet. Roger knew how to build the systems but he did not know how to build his business. Worse yet, Roger did not feel he handled people well and questioned his ability to build an effective operations and administrative team. He felt he lacked marketing skills and had no vision of where to guide his little company into the future.

There is an old adage that holds so much truth. It is, "Without a vision, the people perish." Have you considered how important it is to have a vision for yourself, for your family, and for your career? Have you taken the time lately to review your vision of the future and determine if you see clearly where you are going? Having a vision is empowering. It unlocks your mind and frees it to determine how to get there. Your vision for your future controls your future. Without a vision of the future, you may very well stay lost in the present.

This is where it started to work with Roger. My first questions were very simple. First, I asked him to determine where his industry was going and what trends would affect the services and products that he was providing. If we can determine where our family or, if employed, our company is headed, then we can start to determine exactly how to define where to change direction. For those of us who are in business for ourselves, we must be able to determine objectively the direction our industry is going and how this overall direction will affect our business.

Roger analyzed my request to determine where his industry was headed. He told me that the present technology he was utilizing in his systems would be outdated within two years and the future technology was already being introduced into the marketplace. He also said that the new technology was outside of his area of knowledge and he could not see how he could prepare himself fast enough to become technically proficient to compete with other companies. Roger felt that the lifespan of the new technology was about five years and that it would take too long to shift his operations. So, he initially was still lost in analysis.

I then asked Roger if he would take a few days to look at his talents and skills, and see if he could determine where or how he could apply them in any other industry. I asked him to step back and see if he could discover what his mission could be for himself personally and for his business. Roger asked me if there was any data he could analyze to help him answer my questions. I told him that the data was in him so he would need to simply set aside some time every day to go inside himself and see what he would find in there. He laughed and said that he was probably full of mechanical drawings.

When I think back on my life, as I suspect you have from time to time, I often think about those times when I took a long walk to think about a concern. The farther I walked the easier it was to reach that point when I could finally begin to think clearly regarding what needed to be done to resolve the issue I was dealing with. I love to walk along the beach or through a park and think about where I can improve my situation. The more I meditate on the solutions instead of the challenges, the faster I discover new alternatives and new ways to look at the situation. It never comes from analyzing any data, although this step certainly can be helpful in gathering information.

My breakthroughs always come after I have let all of the thoughts and feelings run through my mind, and then asked myself what is the best solution to each situation. I've also found that sometimes it is valuable to simply give the whole subject to God and let Him have it. Of course, if you are going to give it to Him, you will want to leave it with Him.

My next meeting with Roger proved very interesting. We had agreed to meet for breakfast and the restaurant was overflowing with people. After we spent a few minutes talking about the stock market, I asked Roger if he had made any progress on my recommendation. Roger set his coffee cup down and looked at me seriously for a few seconds without saying a word. Just about the time I thought I might have to say something else to break up the awkwardness of the moment, Roger started to tell me how he felt about his situation. He achieved his breakthrough when he started to tell me how he felt, whereas all of our previous conversations had been to listen to what he thought.

Roger told me that he had sincerely tried to go inside himself and that he had driven to the beach and spent two hours or so just trying to discover what he wanted to do. He said that each time he pushed deeper to find the answer, he saw his father reminding him that a smart man always obtains scientific proof before he ever accepts any premise. Roger said that his father had told him repeatedly that he could always rely on mathematical equations and how important it was to base any decisions on mathematical proof. He said that he had always found making any decision outside of his line of technical evaluation difficult, and never felt he was any good at managing a business.

Roger didn't even know how much he owed in his business, because through fear and frustration, he had quit keeping accurate books a year ago. He said he could only imagine how bad his situation really was. Roger then told me how much he loved to be with children and how well they always related to him. It was then that I came up with my first idea. It was only then that I saw the possibility of a solution for Roger.

While enjoying our second cup of the restaurant's famous coffee, I asked Roger if he had ever considered teaching as a profession. I said that perhaps this was the time to shift his career into a position where he could integrate his training and education with being able to interact with those people he loved to be with and could relate to. I was excited just thinking about the possibility of my idea but my excitement was overshadowed by Roger's response.

All of a sudden, Roger became a new person. He literally beamed with enthusiasm as he sat there viewing the possibility in his mind. Just the idea of the mission, just a vision of the journey had empowered him to unlock joy he had not had in years. Roger had just found his future. What an experience to sit there and watch someone transform.

Roger followed through with his vision and is now teaching in one of our local schools. He has found that place where he can excel and apply his innate skills and talents. I too am forever grateful that I discovered my life's mission and words cannot express the joy and empowerment I feel when I focus on my vision for the future.

It's interesting to look at where our past is controlling us and conquer these feelings through discovering our mission and developing a clear vision for our future. I know a number of families who have sat down together and developed a mission statement for their family and have focused together on their vision of how they can make a contribution in the world and enjoy the experience of teaching their mission and sharing their vision with their children.

A mission statement must define our long-term objectives and serve as the foundation for defining our life's work. Your mission statement should clearly state how you will achieve your mission. Regardless of your mission, if you seek it, you will find it. Knowing specifically where you want to go is the first step in preparing yourself to get there. Only then can you begin to see yourself arriving at your chosen destination.

I hope you will take a few minutes after you read this letter to review your vision of your future and determine if you have a clear mission statement. See if you have a clear picture in your mind of what your life and your career will look like as you move forward to achieve your mission.

My dictionary defines the word "mission" as (1) the special purpose or task for which a person or group is destined in life; (2) a sending out or being sent out with authority to perform a special duty. The dictionary also defines the word "vision" as (1) a mental image; (2) the ability to perceive something not actually visual, as through mental acuteness or keen foresight; and (3) the act or power of seeing with the eye. We can empower our own life, empower our family and empower our business by determining what our mission is and developing a clear vision of what it will look like when we achieve it. Our mission statement will guide us and our vision statement will empower us.

I must sign off now and will write again soon. I am working to become a more effective administrator which requires investing more time in determining where we need additional follow-through. I am looking forward to improving my administrative skills and I will let you know how I am progressing. I also look forward to continuing our evaluation of how to achieve continued growth in our lives. In the meantime, I trust that you are having a great month and enjoying peace.

Your friend always,

James

VIII

ARE WE DOING THINGS FOR THE RIGHT REASONS?

"Our Emotions Can Often Get in the Way"

Dear Jack:

I trust my letter finds you well and prospering. It was great to hear from you and I enjoyed your story about your recent cruise to Mexico. It sounds like you had a great time. We are also planning a cruise to Mexico in a few weeks and I hope our trip is half as enjoyable as yours was.

I have been thinking lately about how our emotions can often get in our way when we are trying to achieve new goals. As I have shared with you, it's often all in the way we look at things. I always try to listen carefully as clients define their business challenges and what they perceive are their solutions. In general, most people fall into two categories: those who take personal responsibility for their challenges and usually blame themselves for getting into the dilemma, and those who blame everything and everyone else for their situation. This initial view of each situation always controls how much additional thought these people invest in attempting to solve a problem.

As promised in one of my last letters, a good example of how this thinking can get us into trouble is to tell you about Gordon. Gordon and his wife Gloria own and operate a printing business and also provide services to help design stationery, business cards and other advertising collateral. They have provided their services to several hundred clients spread across a wide range of businesses. They had achieved a solid rate of growth over the years until they entered into a major expansion program during the early stages of the dot.com explosion here in Silicon Valley.

It all started about three years ago when Gordon first called me. He wanted my opinion as to whether he should lease or buy a large amount of equipment he concluded they would need to become one of the major players in the high-tech and dot.com business communities in our area. He told me that these companies demanded a higher level of quality and different variations in print capacity, which would require that he invest over $300,000 in new equipment and hire three new people to handle his anticipated growth.

After reviewing the figures and evaluating each option to determine how it would affect his cash flow, we mutually agreed that he should lease this equipment. His decision would create an additional $4,500 in monthly lease overhead but Gordon enthusiastically predicted his business would explode through specializing in his new-found niche market.

The next time Gordon called me was about twelve months later. He wanted to inform me that for all intents and purposes the dot.com world was dead and this had created a major cash flow challenge in his business. The majority of his new clients were cutting back on developing advertising collateral, and a number of them had already closed their doors and shut down their businesses. Worse yet, Gordon said that he was worried about a mountain of outstanding invoices he feared he would never be able to collect. He now faced paying off over $400,000 in debts and dealing with whether or not he could ever collect over $250,000 in problem accounts receivable.

But perhaps Gordon's biggest challenge was the importance he was placing on his dream to become a major supplier in our high tech community. He was looking at his situation from an emotional perspective and may have believed that he and his company would achieve greater importance in his community if he could become one of the premier printing companies in the high-tech sector.

He was also looking at the situation with a belief that business would rapidly return to normal in a few months and everything would be okay. Gordon told me his new plan of action was to contact several of the larger high-tech companies and get a percentage of their business. He felt they had the resources and, even though business with the smaller companies was very slow, the large companies would still be spending money on projects that he could participate in.

In Gordon's case, he was dealing with the implosion of a new industry and not just an industry slow-down. He was faced with dramatic shifts in business spending in the high-tech sector brought on by these companies' failure to achieve forecasted growth.

Sometimes our motivations come from root fears. I am forever grateful that I have discovered and eliminated my root fear. It had weakened my ability to see things clearly as well as my ability to deal with people effectively. My fear was a fear of not being loved. Many people have these "root" fears hidden in their subconscious that affect the way they see things and how they make their decisions. It is valuable if we will pray for freedom from any unconscious fears. It will greatly improve our ability to take a different approach to many situations.

My point is that many of us have made decisions based on subconscious fears or emotions that may very well place us in a position where we have raised the probability of failure, or at the very best placed us in experiences of long-term weakness and frustration. It's important to always remember that purpose strengthens and truth strengthens. Whenever there are signs of turmoil or antagonism with self or others, it is time to take a fresh look at the situation. That is the time to determine what needs to be done to return our business and personal relationships to productive, expanding relationships that are meeting our income and emotional needs.

Gordon has yet to recover fully from his initial business decision but has discovered that his business image is not dependent on who he does business with. He has greatly improved his situation by modifying what he felt was important. I recently gave Gordon a list of ten questions to ask himself as he was now willing to accept some assistance in developing a new business plan for the future. These can assist anyone in taking a different approach to looking at business or personal challenges. The ten questions are:

1. Have you taken the time to define what the problem actually is?

2. Have you taken the time to determine exactly what you are attempting to achieve?

3. Have you looked clearly at each situation from a long-term perspective?

4. Is the situation meeting your business or personal needs?

5. Have you considered any other options?

6. Have you considered who could guide you and mentor you through the situation?

7. Have you considered what may happen if you do not change directions and develop a new solution to each challenge?

8. Have you determined if your partner(s) can actually perform what you want them to do in this situation?

9. Do the others involved have a clear plan to meet your needs?

10. Would you be better off in the long run terminating the relationship(s) and shifting your energy in new directions?

As Gordon examines each one of these ten questions, he will be able to apply them to virtually any situation. Many times we are unaware of our motivations and why we are so sure we need to do things they way we have decided initially they should be done. People enter into business and personal relationships for different reasons and often fail to see that these opportunities or needs no longer exist. It's valuable to always stand back from any challenges that may arise and determine if we need to change how we see them. Only then will we be able to correct or complete them.

I must close my letter now and prepare to travel to our offices in Southern California. I look forward to hearing from you soon with your thoughts on how you are progressing. I also hope you are enjoying life.

Your friend always,

James

IX

Can We Overcome Worry and Fear?

"Principles for Building Faith and Confidence"

Dear Jack:

I trust my letter finds you well and prospering. I am happy to hear about your progress and I trust you are prospering in all areas of your life. We are enjoying adding several new advisors to our advisory team and feel very good about the future. It is wonderful to see a vision unfold.

In your last letter, you asked if there was any additional information I could share regarding overcoming fear. I have included some additional thoughts in this letter that can assist you when you find yourself facing any fear. I am sure that you are aware that fear of the unknown is one of our root fears, and can haunt us during our entire life. When we add to this fear the fear of failure and fear of loss, is it any wonder we can become immobilized as we ponder all of the turmoil going on around us and how it could affect our future.

As we look around us, we can see business failures, bankruptcies and company reorganizations that are taking a financial toll on millions of Americans. No matter which political party is in office, our economic cycles continue and millions of families are hurt financially as companies lay off employees in order to become profitable, as well as every time our country becomes involved in a scrimmage with one of our enemies.

The lines for warfare seem now to be not only political but also stem from deep-seeded religious issues. More and more people are thinking about the possibility that we could end up in an international conflict that could bring many countries into a war with our country. Then we add to all of these problems a fluctuating stock market and record-high debt. These are but a few of the reasons many of my clients feel insecure, lacking both confidence in our leaders and in their future.

What in the world has happened to us? We live in one of the most productive societies in the world, where our constitutional rights guarantee us liberty and freedoms unknown in most of the countries of the world. And yet we see so many examples of turmoil and fear. What principles have we failed to understand? What principles are we abusing? What can we do to eliminate the turmoil and fear around us?

My files are full of notes from conversations with clients who are fearful of their future. However, I have several principles we can apply that I have discovered can assist us in eliminating fear. I have been applying these principles in my life for the past ten years and can tell you truthfully that they really work. I will share these principles with you as I tell you about Gary, Sarah and Stan.

Last year I went to a conference on investment planning at the Atlantis Hotel on Paradise Island in the Bahamas. I enjoy staying there because amongst other things, the hotel has a magnificent aquarium I can literally walk through and look at dozens of different species of fish. In addition, they have an outstanding buffet. I should also mention that there is a quaint little ice cream parlor at the hotel that makes super chocolate fudge sundaes which I believe is a valuable tip to remember if you ever stay there in the future.

One day, while walking along the beach, I started a conversation with Gary. He was from Austria and was one of the principals of a mutual fund operating out of Zurich, Switzerland. We talked for about five minutes about the conference we were both attending and about how the stock market had been behaving over the past year. Gary then posed a predictable question. He asked me when I thought the stock market would turn around and start another "Bull" cycle. My answer was very simple and, in my opinion, true. I told him that the stock market would turn around when enough people felt it was time to have faith in the market and began looking at it more positively. Gary looked at me for about three seconds, as only a stock analyst can look at a common citizen, and then smiled and said that I was probably right.

Well, whether or not I am right is not the issue; the issue is that I do understand a major factor in the ongoing condition of the stock market. This factor is that most people are controlled by their emotions, and one of the strongest emotions is the emotion of fear and its opposite companion greed. The stock markets are controlled to a large degree by our emotions and they function in direct relation to how we react to all of the news we hear, or all of the points of view we hear from our friends and family. We either feel we will be able to make money in our purchase of stocks so we buy or hold them, or we feel we will lose money so we avoid them or sell them.

Later in the day, I attended a lecture Gary was conducting on several stocks he was recommending we purchase, and why he believed his recommendations would beat the market averages in the next year. Gary listed 22 different stocks and stated four reasons these stocks should be owned to generate profits during the following year. I want to share with you what these four "technical" reasons were.

The first reason Gary listed was that the value of every one of these stocks was historically controlled by consumer spending. He stated that his research staff had determined that consumer spending would increase by over 9% during the next year in the four countries where these companies conduct their primary operations. He then went on to predict that the 22 stocks would grow as predicted, because all four countries were enacting tax stimulus packages that would stimulate consumer spending. His third prediction was that employment would rise because businesses would have to hire more people to handle the growth within these 22 businesses. Finally, he stated that the stock markets in the United States would not respond as well as the markets in the other four countries because we had too many issues rising out of our fear of war and fear of unemployment.

In thirty short minutes, this stock analyst reaffirmed what I had stated would turn the market around. It will turn around when we feel it's time to spend more money, hire more people and place more confidence in expanding our businesses. It will happen when the investor feels that these steps can stimulate the growth of various companies and the value of their stock.

According to one social psychologist, we are reacting, not acting from conscious creative choice over 90% of the time. Although I have no way of proving this percentage, it is logical that we are spending little time looking for hard answers to issues that are controlling the value of various stocks. It therefore appears that our reactions are a significant factor in controlling the market. This correlates directly with our fear of loss and our fear of the unknown. Only our decision to jump back into the market will get us back into it. This decision can only be the result of our feeling that we can make money because it looks like others are making money. Most market momentum and the majority of market corrections are emotionally driven. Remember that the first principle you can apply to control your fears is to quit reacting.

The next principle to apply to eliminate fear is to choose to change. Fear is an intellectual and emotional habit and, like all habits, can be modified with conscious choice. To a large degree, the results we achieve in our lives are controlled by our habits and attitudes. Sure, knowledge is valuable, and yes we must develop solid skills in each and every area where performance requires that we execute with accuracy and precision. However, when you consider how powerful our belief system is and how much our subconscious controls us, you will discover that we are controlled by our habits and attitudes the vast majority of the time.

You may now be asking yourself how we can change a thinking habit and why emotional habits can immobilize us. You may also be wondering how our belief system produces fear. To best illustrate this reality, I am going to tell you about a woman I met several years ago named Sara. I was attending a conference in San Diego during the time when the savings and loan industry was having many challenges. This conference was being held to discuss how to resell real estate that had been acquired through foreclosure. There were about 50 people at this conference who were involved in one way or another in commercial real estate in Southern California. Some of the attendees were from the savings and loan industry, but a number of them were out of work due to the problems many savings and loan companies were having at that time.

During a coffee break on the second day of the conference, I struck up a conversation with Sara. Sara told me she had been in the appraisal field and was now examining her career as she was very fearful of her future as an appraiser. When I asked her what she was interested in doing, she told me that her concern was her belief that commercial real estate would remain depressed in Southern California for years. She did not see any continuing opportunity in that industry. Her fear was based on her observation that commercial real estate had been over-appraised for a number of years and her assumption that it would take many years for values to find some honest and real basis.

I am sure you remember that the recession we experienced about ten years ago created havoc on property values in many areas of the United States. It was particularly true in Southern California, where it was not uncommon for good properties to sell for 35% below what similar properties had sold for one year earlier.

Regardless of how we analyze this situation, we are looking at Sara and how a habit had created deep-seeded fear in her. Her habit was initially triggered by her desire to please her peers. Its roots were in her desire to please others. Does this sound familiar to you? Her habit was to allow the purchase prices when appraising each property to dictate her opinion of value. She began to believe that the value stated in the purchase price was true when there was no real basis for this price.

One major problem the savings and loan industry had was that they had made thousands of loans on properties that were substantially overpriced. When the market began to retract, they became stuck with these bad loans as many of the properties went into foreclosure. Sara had developed a habit of helping out her real estate friends by agreeing to overstate values on some properties when she knew, as a professional appraiser, that many of these transactions were overpriced and a manipulation of the financing system. Now her whole view of a great industry was clouded by her fears.

From time to time, we should examine if our belief system is creating habits that are fueling our fears. If we can identify habits that are fueling our fears, we have taken the first step toward being able to modify the habit. The solution to any problem is often found when we can identify what the problem actually is. I've never had the opportunity to talk with Sara again, but from time to time I remember her and how her habits were controlling her attitude and how these factors generated fear and affected her ability to move forward within her chosen field.

One of the realities in our lives is that we cannot change anything by worrying about it, nor can we change it by ignoring it. Our fears hide in our mind and then emerge from time to time to create turmoil and often immobilize us. I have seen fear literally freeze people in the moment and block their ability to even speak or move.

Think for a minute about the last time you were afraid and what you did, or didn't do, as you experienced the flood of emotion flow through your system. Now, identify what you were afraid of? Were you afraid of what would happen? Did you fear your situation was out of control? Was it a fear of loss?

I realize that people don't enjoy focusing on their fears. As a matter of fact, most of the time, our brain helps us by hiding the fear at a level in our mind where we will avoid feeling it most of the time. However, that fear is still there, and our hidden fears can affect our ability to take action.

I remember working with a client by the name of Stan. Stan was in his 40's and, for the first time in his life, he wanted to change careers. Actually, his attitude was that he simply hated his present job and wanted out. He had told me the same story two years before his final awakening, and every time I talked with him he would always bring his unhappiness about his career into our conversations. I would listen and encourage Stan to consider developing a plan to change his job, and he would always agree that some day he would take action. But he always had some excuse as to why this was not a good time to deal with this situation.

During a review of his financial plan, I asked Stan if he was ready to develop his action plan for a career change. He again gave me a reason why this would not be a good time to deal with his dilemma. I could not hold back my question any longer. I asked Stan, "Are you willing to let go of your fear of failure?" Stan sat there and looked at me for about 15 seconds. The longer he sat there, the more emotion flowed through him.

I remember watching as tears welled up in his eyes, and I remember what he said to me when he finally spoke. He said, "How did you know about my fear? I am totally immobilized when I think about trying to change careers. You see, my father made a career change in his 40's and his experience was devastating to our family. It created so much pressure that he and my mother ended up divorcing, and I had to quit college for two years and work to help support the family. I am so afraid that this could happen to me and what it could do to my family."

Well, I had finally taken the step I should have taken two years ago. I finally helped Stan confront his fear. Now the question was, would Stan finally take action?

Over the years, I have learned an important lesson. The lesson is that although the principle of taking action is important, there is another principle that goes in front of it. That is the principle of preparing ourselves to take action. After no more than fifteen minutes of reviewing his father's situation, Stan realized that his father had failed to prepare himself and his lack of preparation contributed to his poor experience. Stan immediately let go of his fear and started talking about what he would need to do to prepare himself for change. Within a year, Stan had completed his career change. From the day he faced his fear, I have never heard him complain about his work.

We are always wise to remember that we have to prepare ourselves emotionally, intellectually and spiritually. Sometimes we also need to prepare ourselves physically. Poor diets can impact our ability to handle the stress that always comes with change. Of course, with the wrong attitude, we will never venture forward to allow ourselves to experience the rewards that change can bring to us.

I want to spend more time focusing on my own faith and confidence. I am at the point in my life where I cannot have faith and confidence just some of the time, I must have it all of the time. I want to have absolute faith and confidence in my future. I know that to achieve this, I must build absolute faith in God, in myself, and in those who are supporting me and my plan. It's not easy to move forward into the unknown without encountering some fear. But I know that I am moving forward and I am confident that I will take the steps to achieve my goal. I encourage you to move forward also and build greater confidence and faith in yourself.

I must close this letter now and prepare for today's schedule. Take care of yourself and enjoy the weekend you have planned in Carmel. I hope you enjoy the inn I have recommended. You will especially enjoy the cozy fireplace in your room. I will write again soon and I look forward to hearing from you.

Your friend always,

James

SECTION TWO

Managing Your Finances

X

CAN WE BEAT THE PRINCIPLE OF SOWING AND REAPING?

"The Financial Demise of David and Susan"

Dear Dennis:

It was great receiving your letter and catching up on what is going on in your life. I wanted to write to you sooner but found myself absorbed in our tax season. I hope my letter finds you well and enjoying life. We are well and preparing for a few new changes in our lives. I will tell you more about them soon.

I have given thought to your question regarding what we can do to guide our children during this period of turbulence in our financial markets. Considering that many of them want to manage their portfolios by themselves, I believe the best guidance is to share the same principles I have shared with you over the years as we have worked to build your portfolio. We can also learn from the mistakes of others so I'm sharing a few experiences with you that I have had with some of our clients. You will find the story about David and Susan interesting and hopefully it will give you some ideas you can use for strengthening your own financial plan.

I am sure I will be learning more about others' financial mistakes as I see clients during tax season. There is something about tax season that brings out the best and worst in people. I personally love it because I get to see so many of the people we have built a relationship with over the years. Our tax practice has grown rapidly and we now are one of the largest in Silicon Valley so we really see a cross-section of the people in our community. We talk about all kinds of subjects while we are going over their paperwork, and I get caught up on how their lives have been during the year and how they feel about what's going on.

During the past three years, my conversations with clients have been more philosophical in nature because so many of our clients are genuinely concerned and even afraid about their financial future. Better stated, they simply do not feel very secure. Although these people are for the most part well-educated and living in one of the most affluent communities in the world, they do not feel secure.

I am confident we can simplify our financial lives and be secure. Maybe I have the answer and hopefully it will come through as I share with you how I see the world of business and finance from the eyes of the thousands of clients we see every year. My goal is for you and I to stop and examine where we can improve our own situations, as we are the only people we can change. God knows I have tried to change enough people in my life, but I finally discovered that the only one I can change is me.

Anyway, back to tax season and my story about David and Susan. I have been working with David and Susan for about four years. They initially came to our firm to obtain some tax advice and have us prepare a living trust for their family. They are a really nice couple in their mid-forties who have been very focused on becoming financially secure. David was a systems engineer with one of the global technology giants and Susan also works or I should say worked at a very successful computer manufacturing company.

When they first came to our firm, their combined annual salaries were over a $250,000 a year, plus both had sizable stock options from their companies. Both of them together were earning more than the vast majority of couples in any country in the world. Their combined gross income in 1999 after exercising options was over $500,000. Most people would be envious of their life if they didn't know what I am going to tell you. For after our third meeting with David and Susan this year, I had to officially pronounce them financially dead. Here was a couple with everything in the world going for them, who let it all get out of control and ended up financially and emotionally bankrupt.

Maybe you are wondering why I would admit to you that I failed to protect the people from this terrible experience. Perhaps I should only share success stories—but this story holds so many important lessons. I can't think of a more important way to illustrate these lessons than by sharing with you the story of this couple. What's so sad about this story is there are others like

David and Susan in our community—one of the most economically productive communities in the world.

I first noted David's financial attitude and decision-making process when he told me that he had elected to exercise all of his stock options that year. His decision was based on an internal company report to all of its managers on how well it felt its stock would do during the next few years. Based on this information, David elected to invest $87,000 he did not have in their savings accounts to purchase these options and take on the Alternative Minimum Tax liability of almost $200,000 he would have to pay by the time he filed his taxes for the year. During our conversation about the pitfalls of the Alternative Minimum Tax, he stated, with all of the confidence in the world, he would sell off enough stock the following year to cover the taxes and he would rely on the company's financial predictions. He further said that he would hold all of the rest of this stock long-term and would not consider diversifying into other investments because his company was the leader in its industry.

David had committed himself to his company's stock option program, and was betting a large portion of his future financial security on one company. Ironically, the company would eventually terminate him when it was no longer meeting its profit objectives.

I could not get David's attention when I told him about the importance of diversification nor would he have probably have done anything differently because you see David holds a Ph.D., is an expert in his field and truly believes his wisdom crosses over into the world of business and finance. David's financial demise began because he did not have a well-designed plan created from time-tested principles and proven formulas for long-term success.

Although the principal of diversification is foundational and important, it is not the point of this story. What I want you to see is that the cause of David and Susan's death was overlooked and the lesson lost, as they focused on all of the effects that emanated from the basic causes, and later blamed their financial death on factors which, in reality, had little to do with it.

A simple and basic truth to remember is that cause controls predictable effects, and the first step in developing any blueprint to build your financial or business future is to understand the principles that enhance our ability to achieve predictable results. These same principles should be applied for solving any financial and business challenge and the vast amount of time the effects are accurate to predict. In David and Susan's case, the problem was failure to develop a comprehensive blueprint that would factor each and every element that could affect their financial security.

Later that year, David exercised his options and then Susan called me to ask what I thought about a particular dot.com stock. She told me that she had some "information" from one of her friends who worked for the company. Her friend had been told that the company was about to sign a major distribution agreement with one of the giant computer companies which could greatly enhance the value of its stock. Her statement to me was 'I want to do this so we can make some extra money to pay down on the credit line David established to get the cash to exercise his options. We can't pass up an opportunity to "hopefully" make a killing on this stock.'

I asked Susan what the company's income and profit picture looked like and how much additional business they had in the pipeline. She stated that the company had never made any money in its first two years of existence and had no other major orders for its Internet software in the pipeline. She said that she wanted to use $40,000 they had left on their credit line to buy this stock. She assured me they would sell the shares of this dot.com company as soon as it took off and pay off their credit line.

Although I suggested that she cut back her investment to $10,000, she later admitted that she could not resist betting the whole $40,000 on this tip. Since they were enjoying more income than they had every experienced and the whole dot.com world was exploding with record-setting stock prices, another decision was made at this point which later proved to be a part of the condition that "killed" them.

The following March I met with David again. This time he had asked me if we could meet on a Saturday afternoon so we could talk about some tax challenges. I agreed and as we talked, I found him to be quite worried about his company. He talked for fifteen minutes about a number of unexpected problems that had arisen in his company. His view was that the company's challenges were due in part by political instability and shared several examples of legislative decisions in Washington that had adversely affected his company's performance. Then he proceeded to tell me that his concern was that he would have to sell almost all of the stock he had optioned to pay the

$200,000 in Alternative Minimum Tax that was created when he exercised his stock options because his company's stock had decreased in value by almost 80%.

Simply stated, stock he had paid well over $100 per share for was now worth about $25 dollars per share. His initial decision to place all of his financial eggs in one basket was now creating dramatic financial health challenges and challenging his confidence in his financial future.

You may be now asking yourself how his company's stock could have gone down by over 75% in less than one year when it was a leader in its field and preparing for such great growth. You may be wondering why he did not see the warning signs and why he was not smart enough to start selling his stock when the stock first began to decline. Well, he had to wait for one year to qualify the stock for long-term capital gains treatment. Everyone knows that long-term capital gains tax is much lower than ordinary income tax, don't they? Isn't this the point to remember, the principle to apply so that they could have saved money on taxes? This principle is important and should be applied when appropriate, but this was not the core challenge.

I have determined that the solution to most challenges in our lives is in defining what the challenge is. We should always address the core challenges that are affecting our financial and business life. We should also ask, who are your authorities are and how much of the total picture do they understand?

Let's get back to David and Susan as I'm sure you want to know what led to their financial death and whether there truly is life after death. We are now about one year into the events that created the financial cancer that spread and finally killed them.

During the second year, they experienced two additional challenges. The first challenge was that Susan got laid off and could not find new employment. This created a loss of family income of over one hundred thousand dollars per year. Actually, she didn't look past her immediate job description and refused to take part-time jobs or work for a temporary employment agency which, by the way, could have been a path for employment with her company.

Since Susan had free time on her hands, she was the one who met with me during the next tax season to prepare their tax return. During our meeting, she confided to me that she had lost about 90% of her investment in the dot.com investment but was confident the company would survive and her investment would some day be worth something. Our conversation soon centered on her plan to cut back on their contributions to their retirement account. We ended our meeting discussing Susan's plan to refinance their house and take out another $100,000 in equity to provide a cash cushion should David also lose his job.

You should note that prior to obtaining a line of credit on their home to exercise the stock options, they only had $227,000 in mortgage debt. They had obtained a line of credit for $100,000 to exercise the options and buy the dot.com stock. Now she wanted to expand the credit line to $220,000 which would raise the total debt on their home to $447,000.

Susan was philosophical regarding the failure of many of the dot.com companies in our area but told me that she felt there was greater financial security in the larger companies who she felt would weather the storm. She was further confident that the stock they owned in David's company would return to its former level of value very soon. They would then be secure and everything would be okay. In a period of two years their net worth had gone down from over $4,000,000 to less than $700,000 and their debt had increased from $220,000 to over $500,000. But she still had hope for their future.

When David came in to sign their tax return that year, he appeared to accept the situation and commented that he would have to work another ten years to make up for the adjustment in their net worth. Then I asked him if he would be willing to sit down and complete some planning together and where I could support him. His comment was that his company was anticipating a profit in the third quarter of that year and they further predicted this would raise the value of the company's stock. He felt he would be financially well soon and then we should get together and take a new look at their situation.

So far, David and Susan had gone backwards from the high point they had achieved in building their financial empire but they both felt they had ample time to recover their losses. Many have experienced periods in which their net worth declined, but I ask you to examine when did David and Susan make their first mistake? Was there any particular step, any specific decision they made that started their financial decline and eventual demise?

As a planner, I could list several principles they breached and remind you to address these principles to improve your own financial health. However, I feel it is now important to focus on two principles found in both scientific and religious teachings. These are the principles of cause and effect and for every action there is an equal and opposite reaction.

The principle of cause and effect and the principle that for every action there is an equal reaction are always predictable and control the vast majority of our experiences. When we examine these principles as they apply to each situation we face, we are able to see things in a different perspective. We can then ignore many issues which are not the cause but only an effect.

When we make decisions based on fear or greed, we have to live with the fallout that comes from these two forces. Consider listing each and every decision you have made during the past two years to see if you can determine what your patterns are. Then, determine if you made these decisions from a clear and concise blueprint for your financial future or if they were made for other reasons. Check to see how many decisions you have made that were perhaps based on fear or maybe a little greed.

Now back to David and Susan. They had not violated the first principle for sound financial health. They had saved regularly, invested in stock in a large and well-known company and purchased a nice home in a quality neighborhood. They were working hard to accumulate money for the future and were about to invest a large amount of their savings in one of their most precious assets—their two daughters who were ready to go to college. They had even learned what the second principle for successful financial planning was and were applying it in their financial plan.

Do you remember what the second principle for successful financial planning is? Well, it is to make sure that our savings are protected against inflation and taxes.

Taxes can erode our savings dramatically and of course inflation guarantees that our money will be worth less when we withdraw it in the future. David and Susan were paying over 40% in federal and state taxes. They were storing money in tax-effective investments and making sure that they could benefit from lower taxation through taking advantage of long-term capital gains. They were buying stocks for long-term appreciation and they were relying on their home to also appreciate in value to add additional security against the negative effects of inflation. They did not breach this principle.

Are we getting any closer to where David and Susan began to break the laws that control financial health and financial success? The answer is yes. In fact we have now arrived at the point where you can start to see how cause and effect led to their financial demise. Just as in one's physical health, the financial challenges begin long before the symptoms appear. It may take a few years but sooner or later the weakness generates illness which, if not corrected, leads to financial death.

What David and Susan did was seriously break the third principle for financial health. They failed to accept and follow the principle of diversification. They placed too many of their eggs in too few baskets. They relied way too heavily on the business success, or more specifically the stock value of two companies who failed them when they needed them the most.

One of the companies they invested in was a large and well established company here in Silicon Valley. The other was a start-up hoping for aggressive growth. It is not important to analyze or debate the investment potential of these two companies. In fact, I seldom find more than a handful of people who even know how to objectively evaluate investments whether they are stocks, bonds or real estate. Fewer yet have a clue regarding how to evaluate other investments such as oil and gas leases or precious metals.

What David and Susan did was to bet heavily on two companies performing positively during a market correction. They placed their trust on what others inside these two companies were promoting instead of betting that the principle of diversification will most always produce results. For some reason, diversification is a principle that few people are willing to follow. I see literally hundreds of portfolios and have found that fewer than 25% of the portfolios created outside of our firm are actually diversified.

One well-promoted investment advisor defines diversification as holding large company stocks in different sectors of our economy. While this strategy certainly has some merit, it is not one that achieves much diversification. However, this letter is not on financial planning so I will move on and not devote any further time to this issue but to remind you that failure to diversify created a major weakness in their financial plan.

Abuse of the third principle often leads to abuse of the fourth principle. Both David and Susan abused both principles which eventually led to their financial demise. The law of cause and effect now started to work exponentially against them instead of for them.

The principle of cause and effect established two further challenges for David and Susan because they failed to follow two simple principles for successful financial planning. Now I want to tell you about what actually pushed them over the edge. What actually moved them past the point where their financial illness could have been treated?

Before I tell you about their next unexpected financial illness, I want to ask you a few questions. How much do you believe your bank or your stock brokerage firm is willing to help you when you can't ensure that you can pay back what you owe them? How much time will they give you to pay off loans when they have determined the underlying security is at risk? How much will they help you out if you are out of work? These are questions I am sure you can answer without too much research.

The answer is very little and probably no help whatsoever. This has proven to be true regardless of how friendly they are or how many times they have attempted to loan you money when you were credit-worthy.

So what happened to David and Susan that led so rapidly to their financial death? What additional principle did they fail to apply? Which principle did they violate? It was not the challenge that they encountered when David also received his notice of termination. It wasn't even that they had breached the fifth principle for successful financial planning—always adequately insure your assets and your investment strategies.

Insuring assets includes the use of insurance policies and legal structures for asset protection. It also includes hedging against losses and arranging assets to protect against periods of negative cash flow. One major cause of their financial death was their failure to take action to replace lost income. So, remember the fifth principle for financial security which is to protect your assets.

It was not that David did not attempt to find another job nor was it true that Susan did not also attempt to find work. What they failed to do was face the truth. We do not always seek truth before making a decision and often fail to get past our emotions or point of view, which are often clouded with false assumptions and negative thinking. In their case, they could not get past the emotional roadblock of self-importance. They refused to look at themselves and the economy and examine new options for generating income.

The job market for almost everything is controlled by supply and demand. Both David and Susan were no longer in demand because the companies they worked for as well as their competitors were working to reduce their labor costs and increase their profits. Public companies are often slaves to Wall Street because they must reach their numbers and generate profits to increase the value of their stock. Both David and Susan became a product of change and yet they refused to change. Here lies an important lesson for each of us to remember.

The first signal I received that David and Susan were in serious financial health was when he called me to inquire if I knew of anyone who could provide them with some private funds. Their bank had elected to call their credit line and he only had thirty days to refinance the debt. He agreed to place their home as security but would not agree to pledge any of his stock, which continued to be the sacred idol he worshiped. His comment to me was that when business turned around, his boss assured him he would be called back to work and life would return to its previous beat. However important raising the money was to him, he would not consider selling stock to cover his debt at the bank.

I recommended that he talk with one of our mortgage loan specialists and told him how very sorry I was that both he and Susan were out of work at the same time. Although I didn't say anything on the phone, I could only imagine how challenging it must be to meet their monthly bills considering what he was receiving in unemployment income. It was now costing them over $4,000 per month just to cover their loans.

By now, you may be wondering what happened to the $100,000 they had raised through extending their credit line? Shouldn't this money be providing the insurance they needed for this risk? Well, I have yet to tell you about the decision they made when their daughters' needed funds for their respective college plans. Where do you think they had saved money for their daughters' college expenses? Of course, through buying stock in David's company.

When it was time to send funds to the two colleges, the stock market was in its normal late-summer funk, so David decided to wait for a few months to sell stock and used almost $50,000 of the cash they had borrowed for liquidity to cover the college expenses. It is important to note here that neither David nor Susan were willing to explore options for either of their daughter's schooling for that year. In their words, "We do not want to burden them with our career and financial challenges."

Now, we have to add to the cost of college the cost of refurbishing their bathroom which was a small project Susan thought would be nice to do while she had time to supervise the construction. This "little" project had been started before David got laid off and it only was going to cost them $22,000. Anyone who has done one of these projects knows that it ended up costing more. It actually ended up costing over $30,000 which reduced their cash reserves to less than $20,000 which they promptly spent in less than three months of unemployment. As you can see, the effects of poor financial planning now began to take their toll on David and Susan.

What about selling some stock? Would this not have solved the problem? I remember talking with David for over an hour on September 5th of 2001. He finally agreed to sell enough stock to cover the bank debt plus establish cash reserves to see them through until they could both obtain acceptable employment. Please note that I have used the term "acceptable" and further note the date of our conversation. Before David executed his sale order an event drove his stock down another twenty-five percent which triggered another challenge David had not told me about. Actually, it triggered two challenges for David.

The first challenge was that when David was terminated from his company, he promptly exercised and covered his costs by establishing a margin loan through his broker. At that point the stock was trading at around $18 per share. So, motivated by how low the value per share currently was, David purchased $150,000 of additional company stock. I should point out that David's margin loan was secured by his entire stock portfolio which had been valued at about $525,000 before the September 11th disaster.

Considering that the value of David's holding after September 11th went down substantially, his second challenge was that after the brokerage house required him to pay off his margin account, David did not have enough value left in his stock portfolio to pay off the bank.

David and Susan were now emotionally bankrupt. How could this have happened to them? Why was the bear stock market continuing and where were they going to get some relief? It was at this point that Susan made a decision that violated another universal principle, the principle which states that for every action there is an equal reaction.

You may wonder what in the world this principle has to do with their financial death. Well, think for a minute about the chain of events that have led to their present situation. Think about how David and Susan had gone about their decision-making and what they had placed value on. Examine for a minute when they started their spiral downward and what is most likely to happen to real estate values in neighborhoods where couples are losing their jobs.

Do you now have an idea what was about to happen? Well, here is what transpired. Around the second week of October, Susan called me and asked for my opinion concerning her idea to sell their home to pay off the bank. Since they could not refinance their mortgage and they had very little left in the stock portfolio, she wanted to protect their credit which she felt would be important in starting over financially. She believed they could sell the house for around $550,000 which could pay off the loans and leave them with $50,000 to $75,000. They would be free of the heavy mortgage debt and could rent a smaller home until things turned around. She also added that David did not want to sell any of their stock because it was at an all-time low and this was their only hope for recapturing any of their losses in the market.

Ten days later they placed the house on the market for $549,000 when the law of reaction hit them. Within three days they received an offer and two backup offers. The first offer was for $475,000 and the second offer was for $496,000 with the condition that the buyer would sell their existing home within sixty days as a condition of purchase. The third offer was for $455,000.

We have the principle of reaction operating now on three different levels. The first level is a general reaction to the market of supply and demand. During that period, inventory of homes for sale had risen dramatically thus leaving a very strong buyer's market.

The second ripple of reaction was created by the bank issuing a notice of default on the credit line loan. This notice sent out the signal that David and Susan might be in financial trouble and therefore need a quick sale. The third level of reaction was triggered by their need to accept a quick sale which led them to the conclusion that any subsequent offers would be no better than the first three they had received.

Their financial death came swiftly and they were out of their pain within thirty days. By Christmas they were forced to sell another $50,000 of their stock to cover living expenses. They were looking at starting a new year and a new chapter in their lives with less than one hundred thousand dollars in assets and still no jobs. The law of cause and effect and the principle that for every action there is an equal reaction had done them in. Who would have thought that a couple with everything going for them would be financially dead at the age of 51 and 49? Could anyone have predicted their demise?

No one from the bank attended their memorial. No one from David or Susan's old companies attended. The real estate agents did not attend nor did their stock broker. It was just the three of us who met during tax season to have a short and somber ceremony. It was just the three of us who focused on the events of the past three and one-half years, talked about the good times and tried to find some hope for the future.

I wanted to challenge them then to open their eyes and change their thinking but I knew it was not the right time to do so. I could only sit there and listen. Not once did they ask me to tell them what they could have done differently. Neither of them raised the possibility that they might have done anything differently. Both simply defended their point of view and, sadder but not necessarily wiser, vowed to move forward and rebuild the good life they had enjoyed for a moment in time.

I must close now and give my business some attention. I will write again soon as I have gathered some notes on the subject of improving the management of our finances. Until we can be together, I trust you will be at peace and enjoy life.

Your friend always,

James

XI

ARE THERE FUNDAMENTALS FOR SOUND FINANCIAL MANAGEMENT?

"Action Is Important in Our Lives"

Dear Dennis:

I trust my letter finds you well and prospering. I have been thinking about the subject of financial management and how important it is to everyone at all times in our lives. What I find fascinating is that people tend to become very passive when they lack confidence in our financial markets or in our economy.

When we stop and examine how things work, it is clear that there are two different ways to experience life. One way is to go along with everyone else and experience what comes from their decisions. The other way is to become an action-taker and then our experiences will be the result of the decisions and actions we have taken. As this applies to financial management, we cannot gain profits unless we invest capital or personal energy into a project. We have to take action, and put the money on the line. We cannot achieve our savings goals unless we take action on a regular basis.

You have heard me use the word "purpose" when I talk about taking action. Many have asked the question, why save money for our long-term needs when we have so many ways to spend it in the moment? The purpose of saving money and leaving it alone is to ensure that we will have money to educate our children when they reach the age they will need it. We must also save to ensure that we will have the money to generate income when income from our work stops.

In all the years I have been in the business of assisting people in financial and tax planning, I have discovered several important principles that control financial freedom. Do you know what these principles are?

The first principle is that financial success is not based on how much we can earn over our lifetime but rather how much we will save. Everything else that is important in financial planning ceases to be important if we violate the first principle. According to recent statistics, almost 93% of the people in the United States reach age sixty-five either dead or unable to continue the lifestyle they had achieved before their income stopped. You see, there are only two sources of income other than social security and support from family members. These sources are income from work and income from our investments.

Financial security is achieved when we have enough assets at work to meet all of our financial needs regardless of whether we are working. Currently, less than 7% of the people in the United States are financially secure. This means that the cause of financial bondage and financial death is that the majority of people fail to adequately plan for their future income needs. No one can protect us from this possibility. Only you and I can make sure this does not happen to us.

Do you know the second principle for successful financial planning? Well, it is to make sure that our savings are protected against inflation and taxes.

Taxes can erode our savings dramatically and of course inflation guarantees that our money will be worth less when we withdraw it in the future. It is important to store money in tax-effective investments and make sure that we can benefit from lower taxation by taking advantage of long-term capital gains. We can take advantage of the tax efficiency of some bonds and life insurance policies. We can also build substantial wealth through investing in tax-efficient real estate portfolios

The third important principle is to diversify our investments. Diversification can be achieved between fixed interest and equity investments as well as between growth and value investments. It can also be achieved through splitting investments between large, small and medium-sized companies. Of course, we can also diversify our investments through owning precious metals and fine art.

The fourth principle is to seek professional advice before making your own decisions. I am currently preparing to build a new home. For weeks my wife and I drew pictures, laid out floorplans and considered many variations for both the style and functionality of the home. We knew basically what we wanted the home to look like and how we wanted to position it on the lot. But at some point, we sought out a qualified architect and asked him to assist us by preparing the blueprints that we obviously need to build the house. He also referred us to a competent and experienced contractor who has had measurable experience in building the type of home we have dreamed about.

We did not rely solely on the ideas of the architect but took an active part in the design of this home. Wisdom suggests strongly that we avoid attempting to draw our own architectural plans or to build the house ourselves. Although these professional fees will cost us about 20% above the cost of the home, they are worth every dollar and will raise dramatically the probability we will achieve our goals.

I have no idea why people place such great value on information they get off the Internet or information they receive from the many direct mail programs that promote one investment concept over another. I do not understand why so many try to become their own financial planner when they would certainly not attempt to be their own dentist or doctor. Although, my mother did self-diagnose her illnesses for most of her adult life. Of course when she actually became ill, she would go to her physician. My point is that it is always important to seek out the counsel of a competent professional when considering any action that will ultimately affect us and our family.

The fifth principle for financial success is to insure your assets. Insuring assets includes the use of insurance policies and legal structures for asset protection. It also includes hedging against losses and arranging assets to protect against periods of negative cash flow.

The sixth principle I learned in my first year as a financial planner is that the miracle of compounded interest only works over time. Let's take a minute and look at this principle. We know that money doubles every six years if we can earn 12% per year. We know that money doubles every twelve years when we earn 6% per year as it sits there at work, hour after hour, day after day until we need it. If you have $10,000 and you invest it toward your long-term financial security, it will grow to $20,000 in six years, $40,000 in twelve years, $80,000 in eighteen years, $160,000 in twenty-four years and $320,000 in thirty years.

Two more six-year periods and you have accumulated over $1,000,000 set aside for your future needs from that original $10,000 that could have been spent on a number of items that would be long forgotten thirty years from now.

These calculations get really exciting if you consistently put aside $10,000 each year toward your future financial independence. They are exciting whether you are earning 12%, 6% or even 4% per year.

The principle of sowing and reaping really applies to long-term financial security. From age twenty-five to age sixty-five is a short span of forty years. You can vouch for how fast time seems to go by. Our financial health depends to a great degree on our savings habits and not necessarily on our spending habits. It's only when our spending gets in the way of saving money that it negatively affects our financial health.

My point is that each and every principle can help us if we will develop the habit of applying them. Habits are difficult to modify and seldom can we modify a habit without daily focus on it for periods of at least ninety days. A great exercise to consider is to become a serious saver for the next ninety days. See how much better you feel saving a percentage of your money every month if you are not already doing so. Watch how you start to look at your finances differently when you start to accumulate money earmarked for your long-term security.

Before I go any further outlining how to achieve financial success after financial failure, I want to take a moment and talk about our attitude. More specifically, our attitude affects our ability to accumulate sufficient assets to achieve financial freedom. I find that few people truly believe they should be wealthy and fewer yet have an attitude of abundance. I work with a number of millionaires who worry constantly that they will run out of money. Many of these people have developed serious negative attitudes after they had accumulated a few hundred thousand dollars because they have become obsessed with earning that extra two percent every year or simply fear they will lose what they have already accumulated. Our attitude controls so much of our life experience, and must be examined and often modified, if we are to achieve long-term financial security.

What is your attitude about financial freedom? What were your parents' attitudes concerning money? What does your church teach about accumulating wealth? In order to become wealthy, as you define wealth for you and your family, you must develop a positive attitude toward wealth. This attitude must start with the choice to become financially independent and must also include accepting the truth that you are worthy of becoming financially independent.

I'm not suggesting you become another Donald Trump—only to take control over your financial life through establishing a solid long-term investment program based on solid principles. Replace any feelings of fear and greed with an attitude of faith and confidence.

Start your program of financial security by developing your twenty-year plan. This is most valuable even if you are in your sixties or seventies. In order to develop your plan, you will want to be able to answer the following questions:

1. What amount of income would I need each month if I no longer chose to work?

2. What amount of money do I want to accumulate for specific goals, such as educating my children, or acquiring a second residence?

3. What amount of money do I need to accumulate as part of my long-term retirement goals?

4. How much money would be needed to establish my own business to (a) help keep me busy and involved during the early years of my retirement, or (b) make the transition to own and operate a family business as soon as I have accumulated enough money to start or acquire it?

Make sure that you really want to achieve these goals, and be sure that they are measurable and meaningful. Be sure to record your goals and review them on a regular basis. I recommend that you review them every month during the first year of your plan so that you can improve the probability of modifying your habits and attitudes toward accumulating wealth.

Many people have developed the habit of paying themselves last, when they should be paying themselves first. If we have a budget, it normally is filled with various payments toward debts we have created, and on various items associated with our standard of living. I have found that most people adjust their standard of living to their paycheck and few factor into their monthly budget a percent of what they earn for long-term savings.

I see a number of our clients using their 401k to save money, and this has helped them establish savings habits on a monthly basis. However, few leave their target savings alone for long and seem to reduce their savings budget when the stock market or fixed interest investments are adjusting downward, which historically happens every three years or so. Regardless of their tendency to quit saving when they need to be saving more money, savings through a 401k does help get the money out of their paycheck and into their long-term savings account.

The principle is to pay yourself first, and it is wise to establish your savings goal as a percentage of your gross income. Although percentages will vary due to a number of related issues, your budget for long-term savings must be at least 10% of your gross income in order for you to achieve any real long-term financial security.

I am not going to make specific recommendations, nor am I going to compare the historic yields of different investments. I'm going to share a few thoughts about the order for placing money, which is a different subject. Many people often place their priorities in the wrong order and start taking large investment risks instead of making their first priority building their foundation for long-term financial security.

What comes first for building long-term security? In my opinion purchasing a home comes first. Over the past year, I have met with several clients who have achieved the accumulation of more money than they ever expected they could ever accumulate because their home has appreciated in value during the years they have owned it. Before you start investing in paper or other assets, take the first step and achieve home ownership.

I also like second home ownership as another place to save money for the future because it presents a marvelous way to improve both your family relationships and your overall quality of life. Whether your second home is in the mountains, on your favorite lake, or at the beach, you will be investing in your future and enjoying your investment far more than watching the value of your stock portfolio every day.

The second step is to acquire a well-designed permanent life insurance policy that will enable you to establish regular savings habits, and under current tax laws, enables you to accumulate and withdraw these savings on a tax-efficient basis. Modern life insurance policies can provide you with asset allocation (diversification), and the advantage of the experience of numerous professional money managers. More importantly, the life insurance death benefit will create an estate for your family with tax-free dollars, should you die prior to reaching your savings goals.

After years of watching people try to save money on their own or trying to buy temporary insurance and invest the difference on their own, I have determined that saving through permanent life insurance is a valuable strategy. An adequate amount of life insurance should be acquired before we place money in programs of less predictable investment returns. Regardless of your present marital status, investigate how you can benefit from storing your long-term savings inside a well-designed life insurance policy.

The third place to store money is in tax-deferred retirement accounts. It is wise to put aside a percentage of your annual income into a long-term retirement program and leave this money alone for your long-term needs.

If you then have additional funds to save for your long-term plan, diversify these dollars between government or corporate and bank loans (bonds and certificates of deposits), and equity in real estate or quality securities. In the majority of plans, the smallest percentage of your investment portfolio should be allocated to high-risk ventures.

I have many clients who save regularly and aggressively for items they will purchase within a short period of time. Saving money for short-term cash needs provides many people with a false sense of sound money management.

Include all of the items you wish to purchase over the next two years into your budget, with your long-term savings budget established in front of any of these items. Make sure that you actually need these items before you include them in your budget. Make sure you are not simply buying the new computer or the new car because you are caught up in the marketing hype. and make sure that you don't tie up large amounts of capital in depreciating assets such as computers and automobiles.

Over the past two years, I have watched a number of clients quit saving money through the purchase of mutual funds or stocks because the funds were experiencing losses. I have also witnessed numerous instances where they quit saving money in certificates of deposits or money market accounts because they were so upset over the low interest they were receiving on these accounts.

Whether our focus is on saving through debt instruments that pay a fixed interest or through investing in stocks or mutual funds, remember that everything is cyclical and will change. Statistics show that less than five percent of long-term results are achieved by market timing or selection of specific securities. The key is to keep saving and keep diversifying, and stay free of habits and attitudes that will weaken your plan.

I want to talk about something else for a few minutes. Let's examine how much we were able to learn from the media about the true reasons for the dramatic changes in our economy over the past few years. But before we do, I have a few questions to pose to you. How do you feel about your life and the future after watching many of the news programs currently being aired on television? What have you learned that gives you confidence in your future as an investor or business owner? What answers have they given you that you are going to apply in the future that will guarantee that you will not be a victim of poor planning and abuse in our present financial and business systems?

Which reporters that you have listened to have told you that they saw the challenges coming and how to avoid them? Which commentator has given you a formula to apply so that you can be free from all of the turmoil we have about us? Have you been able to find the answers from these people?

One of the reasons that so many people are in turmoil and frustrated is that they, like you and I, are asking themselves a very important question. This question is why did the events of the last three years happen if those in control were as smart as they think they are? Why did so many people get financially wiped out when there is so much information available and so many advisors who all pride themselves on having the answers? Where did they all go wrong? Where did the systems fail? Who is to blame?

Can we protect ourselves through new legislation? Do our political leaders have any clue as to what to do to avoid the experience happening to us again and again during our lifetime? We have heard a lot about the disasters and we have been told that several individuals were perhaps even guilty of fraud and mismanagement. Yet, in reality, we are all making decisions daily which we believe are right and we further believe will bring us positive results in both our finances and in our businesses. How do we achieve financial independence? We achieve it through applying the principles we have discussed on a consistent and persistent basis.

I must go now, but I look forward to writing to you again soon. I trust you are enjoying life and avoiding the turmoil we are experiencing around us.

Your friend always,

James

XII

WHY DO SO MANY PEOPLE
HAVE SO MANY CHALLENGES
WITH MONEY?

"How to Modify Your Thinking About Money"

Dear Dennis:

I trust you are well and that your life is full of joy and abundance. I have wanted to write you for several days but found myself dealing with several of our clients' financial challenges. I read your last letter and I realize that different people look at money differently. Many of the people I have worked with over the years have taught me a great deal about the subject of money. I want to share with you a few of my discoveries regarding money and what does and doesn't work. The more we understand money, the more prepared we can be to build greater securing in our personal and business financial life.

An often confusing area in our lives is our understanding of money and our use of money. Perhaps you have never looked at this subject as though it were confusing but simply looked at it from the perspective that it often leads one to feelings of frustration. Either way, I have found that few people really understand money and fewer yet have learned that the money we all have is the result of our collective thoughts, feelings and actions.

I want you to do something for yourself you will find interesting and valuable. What I want you to do is to take the time to think about how you value money. How have you valued money in the past, and where do you place money as you think about your career and your current lifestyle?

Do you have any idea where you learned these values? Are you aware of your attitude toward money? Are you aware of your habits for managing your money? How would you define your ability to manage money? My last question is, how does money fit into your concerns about your future?

My files are full of notes I have taken over the past twenty years from conversations with clients regarding their challenges with money. When I think back, there are two people who unfortunately should be highlighted now because they are good examples of what can be learned about the subject of how our attitude about money can affect our lives. Let's name them Ray and Cheryl. When I first met Ray and Cheryl, they were in their early 40's, had three children and a magnificent home on a golf course in one of those country clubs many dream of belonging to. They had worked diligently for over ten years to achieve their new status and both Ray and Cheryl were continuing to work hard to finance their lifestyle.

Over the previous five years, both Ray and Cheryl had worked on the average 50 hours a week not counting of course several hours they both spent at home returning e-mails and reading reports. They both held respectable positions in their companies, and Ray was one of the top producers in his company's west coast sales team.

We are talking here about people making money from hard work and people working because they enjoyed it. We are not talking about Ray and Cheryl because they were in debt, nor are we talking about them because they would violate any of the important principles we have discussed so far. We are talking about them because they worshiped money, or specifically the things they bought with their money. Their entire life was built around their physical possessions. The bigger the house, the better they felt. The greater the amount of art they purchased, the happier they became. During our first planning session, I asked each of them what they wanted to achieve over the next couple of years.

Cheryl wanted to buy a vacation home in Aspen, and Ray wanted to buy a membership in the country club where their home was located. When I asked them how much these items would cost them, they estimated about $400,000. When I asked where or how they would generate another $400,000, their immediate reply was that both would simply work harder and generate more income. Ray would generate his share through selling more components and Cheryl would simply log more hours, and stated with a smile, that her company actually encouraged its managers at her level to work overtime.

It was not uncommon for some managers to work seventy or more hours each week. Both Ray and Cheryl told me that they felt confident they could achieve their goals, and I remember noting in my file how much discipline they both appeared to have.

You may be trying to determine what their problem was, and concluding that this example has nothing whatsoever to do with you. Isn't it healthy to want nice things and take pride in accumulating them? You may relate to the story even though your situation is different. So far, the pattern we are seeing is that Ray and Cheryl are selling out their bodies and their ability to truly enjoy their money, because their focus is always on how many things they want, and what they will have to do to obtain these things. They value the things, and the more things they get, the more they want.

I first met Ray and Cheryl ten years ago. The last time I met with them, I observed two people who had wrecked their health and were emotionally separated from each other because they had burned themselves out physically. Their emotional center was no longer on their relationship but on what they had accumulated. Their value system was the challenge. It had burned them out emotionally and physically and created a life void of intimacy and thankfulness. Although they had accumulated an impressive list of assets, they lacked abundance.

In order to enjoy money, we must possess a spirit of thankfulness and abundance. In order to have a balanced life, we must place money and the entire subject of wealth in its proper perspective. It is so amazing to me when I realize that few people really have a spirit of thankfulness and abundance regardless of how much money they have.

Ray and Cheryl still have time to modify their thinking and discover life. They still have time to discover each other and what they truly enjoy. I do not want to leave the impression that Ray and Cheryl are not good role models for demonstrating the law of sowing and reaping. They have certainly demonstrated that hard work generates its proportionate yield. What we should learn from the example of Ray and Cheryl is that they developed an emotional center (the center of their feeling of self-worth) around their physical possessions. In an effort to feel valuable, they filled their life with possessions but failed to achieve a life filled with thankfulness for what they had accumulated, and the peace and joy that comes from feelings of abundance.

You see, feelings of abundance assist us in enjoying ourselves, and in having peace of mind in the moment, regardless of how much we have to show for in that moment.

Having considered the thoughts I have just shared with you, my question now is, how much money will make you happy? How many possessions will provide you with the security and happiness you seek for yourself? I can tell you from personal experience that one cannot achieve thankfulness and abundance from how many homes, stocks, or office buildings they own. We only achieve this state of mind through making a simple choice right now that we are thankful for what we have financially, and are thankful that more abundance is coming to us, because we know we will reap what we sow in achieving greater levels of effectiveness and productivity in our career.

Does this make any sense to you? If it does, pass the message on to someone else in your life. If it doesn't, consider the following story.

Several months ago I took a trip to Italy. My wife and I go to Europe a couple of times each year, to enjoy its architecture and its food. The primary reason I personally enjoy these trips is that they give me an opportunity to get away and think about my life, and what I want to achieve during the next six months or so. Sometimes I walk along the lake in Lugano, Switzerland enjoying its beauty, and other times I walk around the Louvre in Paris simply looking at the beauty around me and thinking how thankful I am that we can enjoy it. No matter where we go in that part of the world, I am reminded of the past because there are so many beautiful buildings that have been built there over the past few hundred years.

I am forever at awe when I consider how many people have come and gone before me, and what kind of impact they have left from their life. When walking through the Louvre I sense the lives of the artists whose works of art line the hallways and galleries depicting how they felt about events in the past.

When walking through Rome, I thought about an empire that had come and gone. As we traveled through Florence, Italy, we spent one morning visiting the Pitti Palace. I wondered about the people who owned it, as I walked through room after room each designed with grandiose ceilings and lavish furniture. Several of these ceilings were literally covered with solid gold leaf carvings and the murals were so magnificent, one could spend an entire day just soaking in their beauty. More than two hundred years have passed since this palace was built. More than one hundred years have passed since any member of this royal family walked these halls and enjoyed their grandeur.

Throughout the palace we discovered dozens of pictures of the family that had lived there. On each picture, engraved on a gold plate, were the names of the people who built the palace, their sons, daughters, grandsons, granddaughters, aunts and uncles. Perhaps we read more than seventy of these gold plated memorials to the life of each of these people that made up this family.

As we were leaving the palace, we walked out into a garden that seemed to stretch for a mile up several terraces. In the garden, I found fountains with benches where one could sit and enjoy the splendor of the garden. As I stood there looking at one of the fountains, I wondered if all of this made the people who had built it happy. Then it struck me that this family understood how important quality of life was.

Although there was plenty of evidence this palace was built for others to enjoy, it was also obvious that it was built primarily for the family to enjoy. This house and its grounds painted a picture of what this family stood for. Everything I saw told me they placed value in their family, because each room was designed to present the tastes and personality of its resident. They used money to enhance the quality of their lives.

Regardless of where I go, I always attempt to determine if the people in that community are happy, and how they value quality in their lives. If you look for it, you can see it; you can see the answer to this question in their faces if you take the time to look carefully at them. This is what I want you to consider. What would I see if I toured your home? What will I see if I look in your eyes? Will I see that you are enjoying life and that you are thankful for your quality of life? Will I see acceptance for where you currently stand, as you walk down the road to achieve a better life for you and your family? Will I see thankfulness?

When we left Florence, we went to a charming town not too far away called Sienna. The old part of the city is a picture of life 800 to 1,000 years ago. Today the old city is bustling with businesses selling everything from pizzas to Gucci designs. When I walked through the narrow streets of the old section, I had the feeling that many of the people had a healthy attitude toward the value of money. I did not see waste, nor did I see struggle. I saw many people who were thankful and abundant, and were working hard to meet their needs.

As we left Sienna, we passed several well manicured neighborhoods full of attractive homes one would expect to see in neighborhoods in the United States where many of our friends live. I was struck by the reality that these nice homes are owned by people in that community that are working hard to enjoy their life and leave a legacy to their children.

I don't know if there was an industrial park or a high-tech community in their small town. I have no idea how many made their money via the stock market or how many of their homes where paid for by incentive stock options. What I do know is that I saw people working hard to be good business people and I saw people whose eyes told me they felt secure and were at peace. I did not see struggle nor did I see any evidence that they were being economically cared for by their system.

What is my message from this recap of our recent trip to Europe? It is that I am quite certain many in our society have lost sight of the value of money to enable them to achieve quality in their life, regardless of how much they earn, or how grand their homes are. I encourage you to take the time to determine how you value money, and how abundant you feel at this moment.

What else is important about money? At times, our lives become very complicated and we may struggle to find that space where we can feel secure. During these times, we may be seeking something that will remind us we have control of our lives. We may be thinking how important we are because some bank thought enough of us to grant us a credit card. We may feel secure in knowing that if we want to go to the mall, we can pretty much purchase any item there that makes us feel good in the moment. Here lies a false sense of security.

I recently read a rather shocking article. What it said was that over the past twenty years, average personal debt had increased between four to six times as much as average personal income depending on the age group that was evaluated. The author of the article stated that the average person pays out 1/6 of his or her monthly income on credit card debt and the ratio was even higher in several age groups.

I do not know where you stand on the issue of managing credit but I will tell you that many of our clients are in credit card bondage. It is not uncommon to find people who are giving 20% of their monthly income to some bank, to cover the interest on their credit card debt. I am not suggesting that credit cards or, for that matter, the banks are the problem. What I am telling you is that they are a challenge for many people.

We must remember that money is the result of our investment of time and energy into an activity that will provide us with commensurate yield. Purchasing items on credit to make us feel that we are in control, or to feel more valuable in the moment, is not sound money management. When we take control of our credit, we feel far more secure, and are in control of something which has held millions of Americans in bondage for years.

I want to tell you about Don and Michelle. Don and Michelle were referred to me by one of my oldest and dearest clients. The day they called me to ask if I would agree to meet with them, Michelle asked if I was willing to meet with them and her father to discuss their investment portfolio and review their taxes. Although I agreed to her request, I immediately knew we were dealing with a common challenge so many people have with money.

I remember the first meeting as though it were yesterday. I have a sofa and a love seat in my office that are arranged next to each other so I can sit on the smaller love seat and interact with my guests who normally sit on the sofa. When the three of them arrived, Don proceeded to sit down on the love seat while Michelle and her father sat down on the sofa. Regardless of the fact that this seating arrangement left no room for me to join them in this area of my office, I knew immediately what I would be dealing with.

After about five minutes of casual conversation, giving us all time to get to know each other, Michelle's father shifted the conversation to the subject at hand, by asking me an interesting question. His question to me was, could I assist Michelle and Don in establishing a more secure savings and investment plan?

His concern was that a few of the investment decisions Don had made had proven to be poor decisions, and he wanted to protect them from making any further mistakes. I asked Don how he felt about his savings and investment plan and what he thought about the issue of restructuring their plan. Don's response was that he had invested $35,000 of their savings in a couple of stocks that had tanked during the first market correction in 2000. He was about to tell me his plan for correcting their strategy, when Michelle jumped in with a predictable comment. Her comment was that she had been mad at Don for two months for buying the stocks, but realized they were not as experienced as her father in investing. However, she was willing to move forward and establish a plan more like her father's plan. She said that she trusted her father and felt he should be involved in deciding what their plan should look like.

At this point in the conversation, Michelle's father said that he had seen his parents wiped out financially during the 1950's, and he had learned that it's much better to entrust his money with his bank, to avoid any risk. He pointed out that this provided him with a feeling of security, which he also desired for Michelle and Don.

In this situation, we see a classic situation unfolding—one that was already creating relationship challenges for Don and Michelle, and demonstrating a common challenge so many of us have with our relationship with money. This situation is that we fail to take personal responsibility for it and may learn poor money management habits from those who we feel secure about giving us financial advice, which in this case was Michelle's father.

In reality, Michelle's father was a very nice guy who had a simple financial plan, which entailed placing his excess cash into his savings account at his bank. Although he was earning less than 3% interest on his "investment portfolio" at the time we met, he was giving this young couple advice that could rob them of real security for their financial future.

I am not sharing this story with you to illustrate the weakness of putting all of your money in investments that guarantee that after taxes and inflation your money will be worth less when you withdraw it than when you deposited it. I am sharing this story with you to challenge you to take a close look at who you are seeking your financial advice from, and how your results may be affected from this person's capacity to guide you. Also take a close look at who should be the decision makers in your family and how they go about making these decisions, in a way that will strengthen the relationship and not weaken it.

I had the opportunity to share with all three of my guests that day the principle of asset allocation, and how it affects long-term money management. I'm happy to report that all three are now managing their own portfolios in a more effective manner.

But the key decision Michelle made that day was of equal importance to her and Don. Her decision was to let the past go, and work closely with Don to develop a more diversified investment plan the two of them would be equally responsible for.

By the end of that meeting, I felt that this couple had learned a lesson many people never learn, which would ensure that they would achieve greater financial security in their future. This decision was to avoid giving their responsibility for managing their money away to someone else, who may not have sound or responsible input. Although we love our parents dearly, it may not be wise to look at them as our financial authorities.

I have one last thought regarding the management of money. We are all exposed to a particular "need" that has gotten many people in trouble. It is an emotional habit and often very hard to change. Have you figured out what the habit is? Stop for one minute and see if you can identify this challenge.

Well here it is. It is the need for immediate gratification. Has this one ever applied to you? I know I have experienced it in the past. This emotional need, along with credit card abuse, can get us into real conflict with ourselves and others. Take a look at your spending habits and when you are most likely to buy something on impulse. Take a look at how you manage this subject and choose to modify your habits immediately.

The best way to modify the emotional habit of the need for immediate gratification is to establish a plan to tie your purchases to specific income goals. We should learn to feel better about ourselves through rewarding ourselves for achieving goals, instead of spending money to try to feel better about ourselves.

I must close this letter as it is late and I can use some sleep. I am happy to hear about your plans for the coming new year. I am confident it will be another great year for you. I look forward to hearing from you again soon. May you always be at peace and have great abundance in your life.

Your friend always,

James

XIII

WHO IS RESPONSIBLE FOR YOUR RETIREMENT PLAN?

"Thoughts on Managing Your Portfolio"

Dear Dennis:

I trust my letter finds you well and making real progress in your goal to improve your children's ability to make wise financial decisions. We are well and actually enjoying the challenges associated with our expansion program. We have been very busy planning for the next year and buying furniture for our new home in Southern California. We had the most beautiful dining room set delivered today. Life is indeed great.

I have been thinking about the number of people who have seen their retirement accounts dwindle and how much turmoil this has created. I thought it would be a good time to share a few principles with you for managing retirement portfolios.

I was watching television recently and I happened to channel surf to one of the evening news programs. I was fascinated as I listened as the two news commentators interviewed several senators about their proposed plan for protecting our 401k's. It appears that the government has decided that they can legislate the long-term value of our retirement accounts and assure us security for our later years. That is not what they are saying directly, but in reality that is what the public wants to hear, so that is where they focus their concern and their public discussions.

One of the commentators said, "We all know that millions of people who saw their accounts drop as much as 70% during the past three years would support any bill that would assure them that this would never happen again." The second commentator commented, "Something has to be done to stop corporate abuse of our 401k accounts." The first commentator then shifted the interview to ask one of the senators his opinion as to what he would do to protect us from shrinking retirement balances. This senator remarked that many people from his state had written him asking what he could do to help them with this challenge they were having in their lives.

Retirement is on the minds of many of our clients, and I hear increasing frustration and fear as they discuss their future. We are living in very frustrating times as over 75,000,000 people head toward the years when they fear they will no longer be needed or wanted in the work place.

You and I are a part of this group of people. Our lives were first impacted, as we became the first generation to become attached to credit cards. We were taught how easy it could be to buy now and pay later. Many who work for corporations were then taught to save their own money for retirement through their company's 401k plan. It was really easy to begin each year with a commitment to save money for retirement, but of course there were those credit card payments and wouldn't it be better to save less so we could pay more against the card balances.

Year after year we all have tried to save money and in the past few years many people have done much better sticking with their annual commitment to save money for retirement. Achieving this commitment made us feel very good, and of course this positive reinforcement helped us stick to our commitment, until all of a sudden our account balance began to go down in value. Now, some people are asking themselves if saving money through this vehicle is worth it. A number of people have shifted their focus from saving money to worrying about how many more years they will have to work before they can even consider retirement.

No matter how I look at this situation, I still conclude that we are all personally responsible for our own retirement account. We should spend more time managing it and less time worrying about it. The good news is that there are time-tested principles we can all apply to insure greater security for our future.

Over the past five years, I have reviewed well over a thousand 401k accounts. I have looked at the overall quality of the money managers each company has selected to manage the money, and the number of options each person has selected to diversify their savings. I believe that my analysis of these accounts represents an accurate view of the average account here in Northern California. I also believe that I've accurately heard the comments the people have made to me regarding the amount of time they have invested to manage their accounts.

My conclusion is that the majority of these accounts decreased in value because they were poorly managed and not properly diversified. A large percentage of the younger people had placed the majority of their savings in growth funds or had focused heavily on the dot.com and high-tech sectors of our economy. They enjoyed the growth as the growth funds appreciated and subsequently experienced the losses as the market went through its correction because their accounts were not balanced. Without exception, not one of these accounts would have been protected by any of the proposed legislation.

According to research studies, asset allocation and diversification controls as much as 92% of our long-term results for management of yield and risk. Therefore, accounts that were not diversified were exposed to greater losses as the stock market's momentum shifted from growth to value.

The same research shows that less than 6% of our portfolio growth is achieved by the specific securities we purchase or how we try to time when to buy and sell them. Therefore, those who failed in their responsibility to understand how the market behaves and follow the principle of diversification suffered substantial losses.

The only legislation that could have helped them would have been legislation that required everyone to receive the education and pass an exam to prove that they at least understood the principles that control sound money management. The sad truth is so many people make their money management decisions on the emotional level. I am afraid that even with this legislation and the required exams, a large percentage of people might still have deposited the majority of their funds where they felt they would grow the most, without understanding or accepting the corresponding risk they were taking.

It is our responsibility to manage our retirement accounts, and we will feel more secure about our future if we will take the time to improve the management of this important area of our lives. I encourage you to take greater personal responsibility for your retirement accounts and not expect the government to solve your challenges in this important area of your life. It is our own responsibility to obtain adequate information and investigate each money manager thoroughly. We would be wise to invest at least as much time planning our asset allocation in our account as we spend planning our yearly vacation. It is very valuable to review our account at least quarterly and perhaps go over them with a financial planner annually.

Getting back to my thoughts about the news program I was watching, I then began to listen carefully as the second commentator continued to question one of the senators. The conversation shifted to how so many people had been wiped out financially due to holding too much of their company's stock in their retirement account. Although there are examples of corporate mismanagement, or at the least improper promotion of their stock within their retirement accounts, in reality, the issue remains one of diversification. If you are in a plan where you have the option to purchase and hold shares of your own company's stock in your retirement plan, I recommend that you too look carefully at your attitude toward the long-term holding of these shares and heed my message regarding asset allocation and diversification.

My conversations with those clients who have not transferred their investment accounts into our firm have changed dramatically over the past eighteen months. Eighteen months ago, the vast majority of those people fell into two distinct categories. These categories were those people who ignored their account and left most of the money in either a fixed interest account or one index fund, and those who were constantly shifting their money between growth funds or growth stocks in an attempt to achieve maximum growth. As I met with these individuals to prepare their tax returns this year, I learned that a majority of the people blamed themselves for their losses and had lost faith in equities. Many in the other group said they still fear equities and are passively holding all of their assets in fixed interest accounts.

It's important to have an investment methodology. Of course, it's also valuable to have one that has been statistically proven.

I am sure you will benefit from learning about Mary's experience. Mary was referred to our company about four months ago by one of our clients. During our first meeting, Mary immediately admitted that she had focused all of her time and mental energy on her career during the past five years and had basically ignored her retirement account. At the age of 50, she was both concerned about and very focused on what she could do to improve her ability to a manage her retirement accounts. She said that she had tried to develop an acceptable understanding of the science and art of investing from surfing the Internet and going to seminars. However, she found that there was no clear-cut way to select stocks or mutual funds to guarantee results. She said that she had decided to talk with a few financial planners and then select the one who could demonstrate that he or she had made their clients money during the last market decline.

Mary had watched her retirement account shrink by over $100,000 in the past year and felt that the best path was to find someone who knew how to make money in down markets. Her solution was to find someone who could provide her with assurances and guarantees that she could always make money in the stock market.

Do you think you could locate a financial planner who could guarantee you that they could always select the right investments to avoid any loss in your account? I assure you that you would have achieved a phenomenal discovery.

During the last ten minutes of my first meeting with Mary, I told her that we would probably not be the firm she was looking for as we could not guarantee her gains in her portfolio in any market cycle. I also told her that we were not willing to guarantee that we could always make her money in the future. I then asked her if she would please let me know immediately when she found the financial planner or asset manager who had achieved no losses in equity markets during the past three years.

I recommended to Mary that she consider a different approach to solving her challenge. She wanted to know what this approach would be. So I suggested that she first approach her situation by selecting a professional advisor who understood the basic principles for managing money and learn these basics. I then recommended that she examine two or three different aapproaches to portfolio management, and select the one she knew would best fit her situation.

My last recommendation was that she then should work with the advisor to create her portfolio, and that they should meet together on at least an annual basis to review it and, when necessary, rebalance it. I ended my recommendations by encouraging her to replace her need to find assurances and guarantees with the knowledge and relationship that could raise her probabilities for long-term success.

Mary responded to my recommendations with an interesting question. She asked, "Isn't past performance at least one indication of future success?" I could see from her question that she had already got caught up in the belief system of so many advisors. I told her that most portfolios are a combination of numerous stocks, and these portfolios are often turned over as many as three times or more each year. I also told her that most portfolio managers seeking growth will take their gains and move on to other stocks thus starting over the cycle of risk for reward. So, I have found that it is not wise to place your money in mutual funds that were last year's winners before taking a careful look at how these results were achieved. Past performance is not a reliable prediction of future results.

Portfolio management is a lot more complicated than it looks. It's not easy to manage your retirement funds by yourself unless you invest the time and effort to become an experienced financial planner. Of course, not all people who call themselves financial planners have developed a clear understanding of the basics and some planners are restricted by their ability to offer a comprehensive selection of fund managers. But, when Mary left my office that day, she had made her first important decision, which was to quit looking for guarantees and begin preparing herself to take personal responsibility for her money.

After four months of preparation, Mary has a new understanding of how things work in the world of equities and debt instruments, and more importantly, a plan which she helped design. Mary's future is going to be better than her past. Not because we have eliminated all risks but because we have reduced her risk and have increased the probability for gain.

It saddens me when I think about all of the people who have come to our firm seeking financial advice after their retirement accounts have shrunk by 50% or more. I also cannot tell you how frustrating it is to see intelligent people manage their money with poor assumptions and inadequate information. That is why I am so proud of Mary, and I am confident she will achieve a more secure future.

I must sign off now but will write again soon. I hope you are enjoying life and that all is well with everyone in your family. Write when you have a few minutes as I always enjoy hearing from you.

Your friend always,

James

SECTION THREE

Improving Your Relationships

XIV

WILL YOU BUILD RELATIONSHIPS ON A SOLID FOUNDATION?

"A Fresh Look at Relationship Management"

Dear Gloria:

I read your letter with a lot of sadness. It has been only two years since you and Ted went through the Personal Effectiveness Program. We know that every relationship can experience some turbulence but Ted's behavior suggests that he is no longer focused on meeting your needs. It's tough dealing with this now that you are also trying to adjust to living on the East Coast. I trust you can work things out and that you will be able to both maintain your effectiveness with your sons.

I have been thinking about your questions about relationships and where they often go astray. I realize you are concerned because this is your second marriage but I want you to let that go and focus on what's important. I genuinely believe we all do have a perfect "life partner" out there somewhere. Wouldn't it be wonderful if we could find the one we're most suited to long before we muck up so many relationships? Wouldn't it be great if we could eliminate all of the antagonism and anger associated with failing to develop relationships that can ever meet our needs or the other person's needs? Would it be possible to have a relationship that had enough foundation through the individual's compatibility that we could reduce the odds of failure to zero?

I am sure that you are aware that half of the marriages in California end in divorce. The percentages of marriages that survive in a number of other states are not much better. These are not very good averages for building a secure long-term personal relationship. These figures have not changed for quite some time and unhealthy marriages create considerable economic and emotional turmoil. I am sure that a few of our friends have either experienced the challenges that arise from a weakened relationship or have a good friend who has gone through or is going through the experience.

As I have thought about relationships, I have been taking a fresh and positive look at this subject. We are here to learn how to develop and enjoy meaningful relationships but many have failed in achieving this goal. I want to share with you four principles that are valuable for building solid and secure personal relationships while telling you about Marilyn and Donna and their successes in this area of their lives. I also want to share with you some of my thoughts regarding dependency and how it affects our lives and our relationships.

I have known Marilyn for about eight years. She works in the human resources department of one of the largest companies in our community. I remember our conversation during a financial planning meeting about six years ago when she announced excitedly that she had just become engaged to a guy she worked with and hoped her pending marriage would be a lot better than her first one. She said her new fiancée was several years older and she felt certain they had a much better chance for success, considering that they were both more mature than when they both married the first time. She had entered into her first marriage when she was in her 20's. This one only lasted three years and produced no children. Marilyn told me that she had hesitated to get emotionally involved with anyone for a long time, and that she was not confident in her ability to be a good wife because she had never been around a good marriage. She confided that she had no idea what was required to function as the perfect partner.

I could see that Marilyn needed to talk about her situation.

I asked her where I could support her and invited her to share her feelings with me and her plans for preparing herself for the "big event". She shared with me that during her parents' 40 years of marriage, her father had been involved with a number of other women and her mother, having discovered his weakness long ago, punished him for his indiscretion by simply ignoring him and withholding any affection. They simply lived together, as many couples do, without any real communication or emotional connection.

She said that her sister was married but that she frequently complained about the way her husband constantly challenged her opinions and ideas.

Her sister had told her that she wanted to end her marriage but was afraid she could not support herself financially so she just put up with her situation. Marilyn said that was a lousy way to live and she never wanted to find herself in that position. She asked me where she could go to get some basic training on how to survive her upcoming marriage. She said she really loved this man and wanted to learn a technique she could use when she needed to deal with any potential challenges that might arise in their relationship in the future.

I don't know about you, but I have a hard time accepting the idea that someone can apply one technique to fix each and every situation that may arise in a personal relationship. A number of years ago, I attempted to improve my own management of my personal relationships by reading several books. I also attended a couple of relationship management workshops. Most of the ideas were based on concepts that had some merit, but they all seemed to take the position that for the marriage to work, the enlightened partner had to bear the burden of accepting the other partner's baggage. I don't know how you feel about this, but I know, in my heart, that we are not here to be abused in any form by anyone, let alone someone who we go to bed with and wake up beside every day.

I must have failed in my attempts to apply my new-found knowledge in my first marriage because it ended in divorce, but in looking back on it, I am at peace that no technique could have saved it. I also have a hard time accepting that the best path for solid relationships is to just accept the situation or learn the art of compromise. I have found that when this approach is taken, both parties end up becoming antagonistic and often resentful due to their failure to have their needs met. Needless to say, now that you are experiencing emotional or intellectual separation in your personal relationship, you know what I mean because the most important ingredient for great relationships is that both partners achieve having their needs met.

Anyway, I am writing to you about this because I want to provide you with a few principles that will support you in becoming more confident and secure in your personal relationships. I trust you will benefit from my thoughts, recognizing that my credentials are not in marriage and family counseling nor have I ever written any books on the subject of relationship management. I hope that what I told Marilyn will be of help to you or someone you know who may be struggling with a relationship and currently feeling fearful or insecure.

What I told Marilyn was that I had invested about a year examining the foundation of personal relationships and that I had discovered a few principles that could help her improve her chances for her new relationship to work. Marilyn wanted to know if there were any marriage counselors who endorsed these ideas or how I could prove that they worked. I said I had no idea whether any one of the marriage counselors endorsed my ideas, but I knew God did and that was good enough for me. I also told her that I knew that they were sound ideas and that they would work because they are foundational and true. She laughed and asked if I would go ahead and share my list with her. During the next half-hour, I shared with her the following four principles.

1. All great relationships are built on a foundation of friendship which has the following ingredients: trust, truth, acceptance, respect, having many things in common and a desire to be together often.

2. All great relationships are strengthened as each partner has his or her needs met by the other partner.

3. No one in a personal relationship should ever tell the other partner what to do. Everything should be by mutual agreement.

4. No one can achieve intimacy or passion in a relationship without peace. Peace is the foundation for lasting relationships.

When we examine the elements of the first principle, we discover how important it is to build the foundation for the relationship on friendship. We also can see clearly how much turmoil can be generated where any one of these ingredients within the principle are not present. How many times has lack of trust destroyed a relationship? How often have we seen relationships crumble due to failure to tell or face the truth? If two people have nothing in common, it becomes increasingly difficult for one to relate to the other and to the areas in life they each enjoy. Far more importantly, life is great when people can enjoy things together. So, I have found the first principle to be the most important principle for building lasting personal and business relationships.

The second principle has so much dependency on the first principle because without trust and respect, you will not bring your needs to the other party. I want you to consider that without trust, one cannot build confidence or faith in another. Without faith, one cannot build trust and without trust one cannot build faith. It thus becomes a circle of issues that block weak relationships and strengthen strong relationships.

Although we may strive to meet our partner's needs, it is important also to know what our needs are and communicate them to our partner. If we do not do this on a regular basis, we will become frustrated and may very well become antagonistic toward our partner. Once antagonism creeps into a relationship, we have started to erode our acceptance of the other person and this can lead to anger and resentment. So, it is very important that each partner understands his or her needs and effectively communicates them to the other person.

Every time I review the third principle, I recognize how important choice is to us in every aspect of our lives. I have absolute faith that through trusting in our partner to meet our needs we will receive them free of demands or force. When our partners discover they have choice, they are more willing to take action. When we realize that they are taking action freely, we can then enjoy the experience far greater than when the other party is performing just to meet our demands. This is true in both our personal and our business relationships and is an important lesson for everyone to learn early in their lives.

When considering the fourth principle, it is always important to remind ourselves that we are able to achieve peace through choice. We either choose to accept or we choose to judge. We either choose to cooperate or we choose to be uncooperative or sabotage the other person's goals. I believe that the root of much turmoil in relationships is our failure to accept the other person's behavior and their point of view. Only through peace can we expect to take action together to achieve greater levels of intimacy and only then, can get enjoy greater levels of passion for everything we are enjoying together.

To build peace in our life, we must first be at peace with God and ourselves. We cannot find our peace in someone else. Peace always comes from within us. Once we have made our peace with God and have learned to accept and trust ourselves, then we can begin to build solid friendships with others. We must first have love within us and then we can freely share and receive it.

I have recently taken a careful inventory of myself to examine how I stack up as my own friend. I recommend that you take the time to complete the same examination. As strange as my recommendation may sound, I find it fascinating to discover that one cannot trust and accept another unless one trusts and accepts oneself. The same truth applies to the issue of respect. We cannot respect another person if we first do not respect ourselves. If we are not able to truly like ourselves, then it is time that we take a close look at ourselves and determine what we can correct or complete. All we have to do is choose to eliminate the issue and forgive ourselves for what we have done. Then, we ask God to forgive us and we move on. That's all we have to do to start the process of acceptance.

It has been six years since I shared these fundamentals with Marilyn, who took them to heart and shared them with her fiancée. She later told me that before they were married, they invested several hours going over each principle and assessing what they wanted in their lives and what their emotional needs were. They chose to trust each other at all times and always be truthful to each other. She said that she was amazed to discover how much they had in common and how many activities they enjoyed doing together.

Several times each year, Marilyn and her husband Roy review their wants and needs together and work daily to correct any issue which might lead to turmoil in their relationship. They have a peaceful and secure relationship, and look forward to the future together.

I congratulate Marilyn for taking and applying the principles I shared with her. I congratulate her for achieving the type of relationship she could not even imagine when we first talked that day six years ago.

Donna is another of my clients I want to tell you about. Donna is one of those people we all know who is always there to take care of each and every need for everyone in her family. She takes care of her three children and her husband, and she also works 25 hours a week to support the family budget. Donna is an automatic giver. The only challenge in her marriage was that she was ignoring her own needs and resentment was beginning to build up in her. We first talked about her feelings two years ago during a meeting to prepare their taxes. Her husband Frank was out of the state on business and Donna had taken on the task of gathering and sorting all of the information needed to complete their tax return.

When people come in to our firm during tax season, they are often a little frazzled. Few actually enjoy the experience of dealing with the Internal Revenue, so I wasn't particularly surprised when she mentioned that Frank had "dumped" the management of the tax records on her and she really had other, more important things to do.

Maybe you have experienced times when you felt like all of the mundane tasks in your family had been dumped on you, and that you were being taken advantage of. In Donna's case, she had this deep-seeded need to show her love by taking on every task that appeared, and was becoming physically and emotionally drained. I doubt she had ever taken the time to determine what her own wants and needs were.

After we had reviewed the paperwork to complete their tax return, I asked Donna to tell me what she would like to have at this point in her life, if she could have anything she wanted. I asked her to tell me what would make her life better. Tears came into her eyes as she started to talk about her needs and what she wanted. Actually, she began her voyage by telling me what she didn't want which is quite common as we all know what we don't want but few know what they want.

It only took Donna about five minutes to start telling me what she wanted and what she really needed. Her "needs and wants" were private and quite basic, and when she was through talking, she looked five years younger and much happier. I thanked her for sharing her feelings with me and promised her that our conversation would stay strictly between us. I did, however, ask her if she would take the time that day to write down everything she had told me. I then asked her if she would also set aside the time to share them with Frank, as soon as he returned from his trip. She said that she would do that and asked if I had any other recommendations she could use to feel better about their situation. It was at that point that I briefly gave her the four principles I have shared with you.

When I was finished going over the principles, Donna really got excited and said that she was going to plan a weekend "get away," so she could share these with Frank and they could make their wants and needs list at the same time.

Donna has turned this area of her life around and told me a few weeks ago that she and Frank organize a few days every six months now just to get away from everything and review their mutual goals and needs. She told me that life has never been better and how much confidence she has in their future together.

I encourage you to take these four principles and embrace them in your personal relationship. Invest the time to determine what your wants and needs are and what needs to be corrected or completed in your life to enjoy a life filled with joy and happiness. Examine your relationships and see how they measure up to each principle.

Not all relationships were born in heaven. Not all have the potential to build a lasting union or the potential for long-term security. We cannot have peace and turmoil at the same time. Since all great relationships are built through a foundation of friendship, we can also strengthen them through applying a number of the principles I have shared with you. It's our responsibility to take action to correct or complete relationships that are not in alignment with these principles.

I must close now and prepare for a trip tomorrow to Cancun. I trust that you are at peace and making progress in all areas of your life. Do not hesitate to write should you need additional support during this period of challenge.

Your friend always,

James

XV

WILL WE EVER FIND THAT PERFECT RELATIONSHIP?

"Principles for Improving Personal Relationships"

Dear Gloria:

I enjoyed your last letter and acknowledge you for your decision to avoid the living arrangement Ted had proposed. It appears that there is an issue concerning values which does complicate your situation. You need to determine exactly what you want to communicate to him now and trust you can reach some new agreements that will meet both of your needs.

I have never told you that I have also had such an experience, as I have never wanted to admit to anyone that my heart had been broken. Would you ever want to admit you had failed in one of life's most important experiences? I have to admit that I had a failure in my first marriage, and I hope that you will learn something from what I want to share with you.

It doesn't matter whether I or the other person was right or wrong. We experienced failure in our marriage primarily due to our inability to meet each other's needs. But it was also a failure in our ability to agree as to how to manage careers and money in a way that would create harmony and peace.

I am an eternal optimist and always thought I could handle each situation. She was an eternal pessimist and often looked at our situation negatively. I wanted to grab the brass ring and run with it and excel in business, but she wanted me to take the safe path vocationally and get a "secure" job. I wanted to travel and enjoy our abundance and she wanted to stay close to home and be with her friends. It can be gut-wrenching to try so hard to fix things and find that the harder you try, the worse it gets.

Since I have agreed to share experiences along with any principles I have discovered, I am sharing this personal story with you instead of talking about someone else because I know so much about this couple. I can provide you with personal insight that can help you make sure your heart will never break. I still get tears in my eyes when I look back on how stupid I was. I guess I wasn't stupid, I was just blind.

I know there are millions of people who are experiencing some struggle in their relationship over differences in opinion as to how to manage careers and finances. As I have previously stated, money can be one of the key challenges in personal or business relationships. However, more then ever, everyone should take dominion over their fears and be able to have faith in their financial future.

Our financial future is always tied directly to our career or our spouse's career. So, if we are worrying more about our own family's finances, or our current concerns are focused on our career or our spouse's career, then we should review each situation and determine what we need to do to correct or complete it.

I grew up in a middle-class family that never had an abundance of money. Even so, I remember that we always had a comfortable house and our family took a four-week vacation every year. I especially remember going out to dinner every Sunday. I was never financially deprived and when it was time to go to college, my parents were able to help out with my educational expenses. But most of all, I remember what my parents valued most, and that this was foundational in their personal relationship as well as in my father's career. You see, he was a minister and that position and his contributions to God's work here on earth were what he valued the most.

Fortunately, my mother built her life around her role as his partner even though he was the one up in front of their parishioners each week. I remember that in the twilight of their lives they were still working closely together visiting the people who where ill and dying. I believe that in the last year of their ministry together, even in their late 70's, they visited over 2,500 people in the hospital.

I share this with you because their relationship and their life's work were tied to their spiritual life. This produced a successful partnership that lasted for over sixty years. It lasted because they had shared the same values. They figured out how to support each other and had the same values. Their values provided them with a solid image of self and their faith carried them through many tough times. Although I was not very involved in their religion, I am forever grateful that I grew up in that family, and I do realize that they taught me so much by their example.

I said that I felt stupid when I thought about how blind I was as a young man. I was blind because I never really understood my first wife's needs, nor did I take the time to help her determine how she could overcome her fears and build faith and confidence in herself. I am aware that we all learn from experience. If we can look at it clearly, we can determine what needs to be done to fix things, if they can be fixed. During that relationship, I failed to look at our issues and I clearly did not know how to fix them.

I was married in college and started my career before I was twenty-one years old. I never questioned what I was going to do with my life, as it was simply in me. I knew from the time I was twenty what I enjoyed doing. I was buying properties and taking investment risks by the time I was twenty-six, and by the time I was thirty I had already started to shift my values to my possessions. Sure I loved my family and yes I did try, very hard, to be a good husband, but I loved the game of business and over time I began to build my image of self on how large my net worth was.

I slowly became nurtured emotionally by the projects I took on every year. The more risks I took, the more insecure my wife became. The wealthier I became, the busier I became, and suddenly at the age of forty, I found myself surrounded by substantial wealth but no personal life. You see, I was emotionally separated from my spouse and simply could not find my way back to a place where we held the same values.

Our failure to ground our relationship in the same values became our undoing. In the final chapter of our marriage, she was not there for me when I needed support, and I was not there for her because we simply did not have the same values. We had been together as a family unit for twenty years and she was a very nice person. She also was a good person and an excellent mother. But we never really knew each other because we did not take the time to determine together if our value system would be compatible before we married. We never stopped to determine our core spiritual or emotional needs, nor did we take the time to understand what each one needed to learn and where each of us desired to excel in life.

We have a mutual friend who is struggling with how to fix failed relationships with his children. You know about Curt and his situation with his son Todd. We never talk about our other friends much because it isn't a good idea to talk about others unless we are involved in supporting them through a situation they may be dealing with.

I know that Curt has asked you to assist him in opening up communications with Todd since they haven't talked with each other for three years. I also know how important you have been to Todd and I know that he will listen to you. What I also know is that Curt and Todd need to work this out by themselves. I think they are simply dealing with the reality that nether lived up to the other's expectations when Curt and Martha separated.

If you will remember, they had agreed to a trial separation before they finally divorced. I also recall that Todd was very outspoken about why they needed to patch things up. Curt wasn't very cooperative then and basically told Todd that he was the only reason they got married in the first place. I'm sure he regrets his statement but I'm also sure he blamed Martha's pregnancy on their decision to get married. They aren't the first people in the world who have found themselves in that situation and they certainly won't be the last ones either.

According to Curt, he simply wanted to help and felt that his dad was just going through some mid-life crisis. But, according to both of them, some hurtful words were spoken. I don't know what was said and it's not really important now, but both of them have yet to forgive each other and probably haven't forgiven themselves either for how they behaved.

We can help them deal with their situation. All it will take is for each one to forgive himself first and then the other. I know that they are quite different people and don't see most things the same. I also know that neither understands the other, nor has the slightest idea how the other person feels. I want to ask each of them if they would write each other and tell each other how they feel and what they want in the relationship. I see this as the first step. What do you think about this approach?

We can ask them both if it is now time to forgive themselves for the entire incident. In most cases, we are punishing ourselves as much or even more than we are attempting to punish the other party. It isn't always possible for the adult to be the person who will take the steps that are necessary to heal the situation.

It isn't always easy for the child to be the one to initiate the communication either. Many times children feel that they have let their parents down and this compounds their unhappiness with themselves. What is in highest purpose now is to ask them if they are ready to choose a new direction regarding this situation, and ask each one if he will take the first step and forgive both of them.

While we are asking each of them to forgive themselves, we should also suggest that they forgive God. I have found that a number of people are mad at God for situations they created and have lost faith in Him because they feel He has let them down. Only after they have forgiven self and God can they forgive each other.

If you will talk with Todd, I will talk with Curt. Maybe together we can help them heal their relationship. Once they begin listening to each other, they can find a new level for their relationship. This is the first step in repairing any strained relationship between parents and their children.

I want to close this letter with a few final thoughts about relationships. Before we can eliminate any financial challenges in our marriage, it is always valuable to stop and examine where our value systems are and what our needs are. The first step is to determine what is most important to us. We should then make a list of all of the things we do, what interests us, how we are spending our time and money, and where we are focused when we take a break to focus on ourselves. What provides our sense of security? Where is our sense of importance? Where is our emotional center?

After we have completed these steps, we should write a mission statement for ourselves and then for our marriage. That's right, prepare a mission statement. We should include in our mission statement our mutual values as well as our career and financial goals. Also include what we will apply as the foundation for our decision-making and how we will go about laying out financial goals that will meet each other's needs. We should take a close look at what we both want out of life and where we place our faith and trust. Without trust, we cannot have intimacy in a relationship. Without faith, we will often have fear.

After years of blindness, frustration and denial, I finally decided to examine myself and discover what I could do to achieve strength and peace in my relationships. Sure, my examination was painful and yes it took quite a bit of time and effort to get to the bottom of my issues. When I look at the day my life was changed forever, I remember that it involved making a simple choice. My choice was to change my values and build my new life on the principles God has given us to better enjoy our relationships and to achieve greater harmony and abundance in our finances.

We are living in a time when a lot of what we hear and read about are people reminding us that relationships seldom work and that financial success is tied to overwork, insider information and taking advantage of others. We seldom hear about people who have relationships that are in harmony— and seldom yet do we hear about people who have mastered managing their finances free of fear and greed.

If you decide to work on this area of your life, you will discover that it will forever change the way you manage money and, in the final analysis, start you down the path to financial freedom. Many people tell me that by improving their ability to communicate and plan more effectively with their personal partners, they can improve their ability to make financial agreements together and avoid upsetting discussions concerning their family finances.

Each person in a relationship has financial wants and needs. Importantly, both partners must be able to express their needs and, more importantly, know their needs will be met. We also have other needs that should be expressed and met. I feel it is important to review our partner's needs often and also learn to share our own needs.

I must close now and prepare for the day's activities. I hope you are enjoying life and will be able to achieve peace and harmony in your relationship. I look forward to hearing from you soon. Until then, I trust that you will remain confident that you will find solutions to your present challenges.

Your friend always,

James

XVI

CAN WE TEACH OUR CHILDREN TO BECOME CONFIDENT AND SECURE?

"Steps We Can Take to Support Our Children to Become Secure Adults"

Dear Gloria:

It was so good to hear from you. I am confident you and Ted will be able to make new agreements that will meet both of your needs. I realize this can create a strain on the children. I trust my letter finds you enjoying life and growing in abundance.

I enjoyed hearing about your trip to visit your mother and I am glad to hear she is doing well. One day, during the last two months my mother was alive, I took a few hours to just be with her and hopefully console her as she prepared to take her next journey in life. She was dying of cancer and knew her days were now numbered.

I remember the two of us sitting in her front room together, talking about how much she had loved my father and how much she loved their life together. We talked about things we had experienced in the past, and events that she remembered. Even at the age of 82, her memory was very clear and she still had such a youthful manner, you would have thought she was years younger. What I remember most about that day was our conversation about her desire that I stay close to my children and continue to guide them.

As we talked, I realized that we would be together only a few more times, and hoped I could say all I wanted to say before she left. But that day was her day to tell me what was in her heart. Paramount in her mind was her confidence in her future as well as her desire to make sure I would continue to guide my children. As I look back on our conversation, I remember that there were no "if only" or "I'm sorry" in our conversation. I recall her saying how happy she was that I had found my path in life and that I was happy and at peace with myself. My memory of that day will remain with me forever. I will always remember how much faith she had for her pending journey and how confident and secure she was.

As I share this experience with you, I think about my children and what I perceive is their current level of confidence and security. I think about them as children, but realize they are now all adults and I can't be there to take care of them. I also realize they must now take responsibility for themselves. I must now trust that they will make their own decisions and that these decisions will be sound decisions. Whenever I have even the slightest degree of concern, I remind myself that I can still guide them.

Do your children currently have a clear sense of direction in their lives? When you listen to them, can you determine their interests, what their attitudes are and their current level of self confidence? Are you supporting them effectively as they strive to become independent adults?

A number of my clients are worried about their children and a few have feelings of frustration and even guilt when they think about their children's future. These people are just like you and me. They really love their children and want to make sure that they become confident and secure adults. They are now seeing their children struggle with feelings of doubt and insecurity. I have also observed that my children have recently shared concerns about their future. What I want to share with you in this letter are four steps we can all take to ensure that our children will be able to achieve greater levels of confidence and security.

If you will carefully observe each of your children, you will find that by a very young age you can begin to see very clearly what their core personality is. I'm not talking about how friendly or outgoing they may be, but their degree of assertiveness and responsiveness compared to others around them. Watch how one child dominates conversations, and tries to boss the others. Look at who is more introspective and reserved. See if you can determine what each child enjoys doing, which is analytical and who is the most amiable. Soon, you will see that each one of your children sees life and attempts to handle their challenges differently.

We are all born with a unique mix of what I will call traits that basically serve as the foundation for our behavior. Each individual also has different talents and skills. Our traits determine how we handle ourselves and attempt to manage others as we face each new situation we encounter in our lives. So, if we can determine our child's thinking and feeling personality, as well as what their core talents are, we can then begin to guide them in a direction that will build their sense of confidence and security.

One of the key ingredients for both feeling and thinking we are secure, is our sense of confidence in how we handle each situation we are confronted with. The more we use our innate talents and skills, the greater the probability we will perform well and therefore build our sense of confidence in ourselves.

Although it is good to encourage our children to experience new things and overcome their fears, it is important not to push a child to compete in areas where he or she lacks the basic interests and talents. This would result in the child not feeling confident and secure following such an experience.

The first step is to discover what your child's natural talents are and where his or her innate interests lie. Then focus on developing these talents without asserting your will or your "personality" too heavily. We all know that we are all dependent on our parents during the early stages of our lives. What we often fail to consider is that each child must be helped to develop his or her own ability to think and feel free of dependence on either parent. This is true regardless of the child's age. Many are still dependent on their parents regardless of their age, and this affects their sense of security and confidence.

Begin today to start looking for your children's innate talents and skills, and help them discover what interests them. Will this ensure that they will grow into confident and secure adults? Their chances will be greatly enhanced if you will focus carefully on step number one.

As we work to discover our children's innate talents and skills and what interests them, we have to deal with our own talents and skills. This includes our ability to be patient, accepting and understanding. Consider for a moment my two acquaintances Mike and Jerry. I first met both of them during the years my two sons played Little League baseball. I think they were about the age of nine and eleven when I suddenly found myself in a new experience. This experience was coaching their Little League baseball team. I knew very little about the art and science of teaching these young boys how to be good baseball players, which led me to conclude that I would focus my team members on building confidence in themselves and in just enjoying the game.

Anyway, about the third game on our calendar, I met Mike and his son Ronnie. Mike was the coach of the opposing team and a talented coach by both occupation and innate talents and skills. His son Ronnie was an absolute natural ball player and had been taught the basics since he was old enough to hold a bat and glove. I watched as Mike interacted with Ronnie, as well as the other boys on his team. He always guided each boy in a professional manner, and reinforced each fundamental with a spirit of calmness and patience. Every time they would make a mistake, which at that age was often, he would let them know it was ok and help them refocus on what to do the next time they faced that particular situation. I learned a lot that day about coaching and admired both Mike and his son Ronnie's talents and skills.

The next week we played another team that was coached by Jerry, who had a son Gary playing on the team. Jerry spent most of the game yelling at Gary without addressing him by name. Gary had very little talent or skills as a baseball player, and Jerry had less talent and skills as a coach. Jerry was a very competitive ex-baseball player who was trying to relive his life through his son, who appeared to have little interest in the whole subject. The more Jerry got worked up about Gary's play, the more awkward Gary became.

My point in telling you about Mike, Ronnie, Jerry and Gary is to simply demonstrate how important it is for you and I, as parents, to both identify our children's innate skills and talents, as well as focus on how we can be a better coach and guide them to participate in activities where they have a chance to excel. So, step number two is to stop pushing and start coaching.

After that season of coaching of my sons' Little League baseball team, I was "retired" to the position of President of our league. I guess this was the best place to get rid of me as I knew little about coaching baseball. I got the job of interacting with several hundred parents which would probably have driven me absolutely crazy, if it were not for being able to get to know a number of great kids who simply were out there to have a good time. It was during these two years that I learned about how to take the third step. Actually, I didn't know I had learned it then until I looked back on those years and saw how important the step was as I worked to support my own children during this period in their lives.

My two sons Michael and Mark both enjoyed playing baseball. One year Michael decided he would become a pitcher. For several games, he worked hard at this position and survived all of the games he pitched in, without giving up too many runs. However, although Michael had been very serious about this position, he was not a natural pitcher so he lost interest in that position and shifted his focus to playing another position on the team as the season unfolded.

Mark, however, would play any position, simply to be able to play the game. He took the whole experience less seriously than Michael, and placed less pressure on himself. Michael was his own judge of how he was doing, and worked hard to be the best he could. He was always good at whatever he did, but never the best player on the field. No matter how hard Mike tried or how hard he worked at any position, he would not achieve the level of success he felt he should achieve.

On the other hand, Mark took a far more casual approach to the whole experience and played the game mostly to have fun. Mark would not push himself, although he was a natural ball player and could have been outstanding if he would have chosen to take the game more seriously. As I watched both of them play each game, I developed a special appreciation for both boys and always enjoyed their performance, even though I did try to help one become more intense, and the other one to relax and just enjoy the game.

During their third year of playing Little League baseball, they decided to form a band with two other young men they played baseball with. If you have ever experienced being a band parent, you can appreciate what I am now going to tell you. The band practiced for hours every day, and the longer they practiced the louder the music seemed to get. It took very little time to discover that both of my boys were natural musicians, and absolutely loved what they were doing.

Mark played the drums and we could just feel his energy and enthusiasm radiating strongly every time he played them. The one who had played baseball so casually was now an intense drummer. His intensity immediately set him apart from other drummers with less passion, and helped him build self-confidence and an appreciation for excellence.

Michael played the guitar and rapidly taught himself to become one of the finest musicians in the area. He loved to play, and was always totally relaxed and full of confidence. What a different experience than his days on the pitcher's mound. He had found his passion and quickly discovered that his talents were in the field of music.

As both of them excelled in their new found love, they became skilled musicians and, more importantly, they became confident young men. They loved playing in the band, and the audience, often filled with young women, loved to come to hear them play. They quickly turned an interest into a business and both have excelled in that field throughout their adult lives.

So what did I learn? What is the third step we can take to support our children to become secure adults? What I learned was that we must guide our children to discover where they can apply their talents and skills. This becomes easy once we help them discover their passion.

If I would have denied them the opportunity to practice with their band, even though it could drive one to drink, they may not have ever discovered this passion that was in them, just waiting to be discovered. If I would have forced them to focus all of their time and energy on baseball, I would have blocked them from discovering what they truly loved to do.

Look carefully at each of your children and when you see that spark of interest and the willingness to invest hours playing or studying in whatever field they have discovered, just stand back and rejoice, for you have helped them take one of the most important steps in their young life—the step to help them discover their passion.

How does that old saying go? Is it "Do what I say, not what I do" or is it "Don't do what I do, do what I say"? I can never remember which way it goes and have no idea where it came from, but I do know that either way, it holds the key to numerous conflicts between parents and children. Where are we in our quest to find our own passions, and in applying our talents and skills to these passions? What are we demonstrating to our children? Is our level of passion affecting what we are saying? Are we casually sliding along through life, just hanging out and trying to keep busy enough to meet our financial obligations, or are we demonstrating how great life can be when we are in highest purpose? What example are we setting for them?

You may ask me why I am placing so much responsibility on you and me now in this letter as I write about our children and their personal security. The reason is that they learn so much from us. They do what we do, and often say what we say. So perhaps the first step for you and I to take to become a more effective guide to our children is to choose to be in highest purpose and discover our own passions.

During the time I was watching my boys play ball and participate in their band, I was also working hard and dealing with my own challenges. In looking back on this period of my life, I am sure that I was not as effective a guide as I could have been to them, because so much of my focus was on my own challenges. I have also wondered just how much my example then has affected them as they grew older. What I do know is that my behavior during the early stages of their lives is certainly embedded in their subconscious, and will serve as a reference point for their view of life forever.

I am sure I taught them how to be a "workaholic", or maybe how to avoid being one. I am also sure I taught them something about relationships, and I know that I affected how they value money, as I perhaps unwisely attempted to show my love through how I spent it. Well, here we are several years later and I now have different reference points from which to build my life and my relationships. Can I still make an impact on them? Can we all still become effective guides no matter how we have handled the job in the past? The answer is yes. We can help them change their lives by changing ours.

We both know people who have both a career as well as children to raise. Most of these people are working hard to meet their financial obligations, while also working to be the best parent they can be. I am sure that they sometimes wonder if they are a good parent, and may even feel a little guilty due to the amount of time they spend working.

If we ever feel a little guilty, then my recommendation is that we examine the following areas of your life. The first area to examine is to determine the level of our own confidence and security. What is the foundation for our security? When we think about our security, who or what do we think about? Who do we have faith in? Who do we absolutely trust? In which area of our life lie our peace and our interests? Our children already know whether or not we are confident and secure. They can sense it in us.

When we have the answer to where our confidence and security lies, we then must focus on where our passions lie. What are we passionate about? Who are we passionate to be with? What makes our work so enjoyable or, if it isn't enjoyable, what would make it so? How has our financial situation affected both our sense of security and our passions? How are we channeling our talents and skills? We should take the time now and answer these questions. We shouldn't put them off because we are busy or would prefer not to have to deal with them. Whatever passions we have will show through and our children will see them.

How are we applying our talents and skills? Who or what receives our focus and attention? Are we making a real contribution in our career or just showing up and keeping busy? Are we hiding out during all of the time we are spending doing tasks or are we caught up in the beauty and excitement that emits from making a real contribution to something we love to do?

Where is our heart? What are our emotions grounded in? The best leaders know clearly what they want and what they need, and then focus on working hard to help those around them discover their wants and needs. Once we, as leaders, have helped other people start to become aware of these answers in life, only then can we work to help them fulfill them. This entire process of discovery and leadership also applies to our relationship with our children.

It is never too late to discover joy and peace as we free ourselves from the limitations that result from our failure to, or fear of, discovering our purpose. This discovery will change our life and assist us in guiding our children.

I must close this letter now and prepare for the coming week. I am aware that little of what I have written tonight deals with specific ways to improve your relationship with Ted but my thoughts can help you in other ways. I also want to share some thoughts about dependency as your boys will be reaching the age soon when you will need to be prepared to guide them away from this challenge. Until then, I trust you will be at peace and prosper.

Your friend always,

James

XVII

ARE YOU DEALING WITH DEPENDENCY?

*"Principles for Supporting People in Our Lives
Who Have Dependency Challenges"*

Dear Gloria:

I trust my letter finds you well and enjoying all of your sons' sports activities. I am enjoying life and finding new opportunities all around us.

You raised the question in your last letter regarding your concern about the possibility your son may be experimenting with drugs. Last week I had a long talk with a client who has a drug dependent child. This situation has created so much turmoil in their family. During our conversation, I was asked how to protect people we love from becoming dependent on any substance or any relationship that would lead to weakening them or worse yet, their destruction. It led me to examine exactly what can be done considering how dependency can control anyone so dramatically. I want to share my thoughts with you to enable you to deal with this situation should it ever manifest itself in your family.

I believe the answer concerning how to help them seems to vary with the age of the dependent person and what has led to that dependency. I know it is important to anyone in this situation to be able to cope with it and to assist in eliminating this turmoil from their family. We also need to know how to guide our children to enable them to avoid this experience. This is a life experience we all want to avoid. We want to have confidence that we are doing the best job possible in guiding our family members away from this area of life that has destroyed so many people of all ages. It is therefore valuable to examine what principles we can apply to remove unhealthy dependencies from our loved ones.

Although there are a number of interesting areas where dependency can develop, I am frequently asked about drugs, why drugs are so dangerous,

117

and what can be done to help others to conquer or avoid them. This challenge is always far more stressful when the dependent person is someone in our own family. We never know why anyone could become dependent on a drug or exactly when dependency begins. But we do know that when this does happen, we see that person losing the ability to control his or her choices. Choice is the one thing God has given us that we should guard with our lives and always embrace its value to us. So, I see any dependency as a challenge for everyone because without applying choice, we are destined to become dependent on someone or something else. This can weaken us, and weakness does not support highest purpose in our lives.

When we look at the subject of choice, we see that first having the desire to change it is the only way to change things. Unless we choose to change something, it will remain with us. I like to think of this as the central element for creating our future and correcting our past. It is the one element in our life that we should always protect and apply when needed.

In our relationships, we have the choice to accept or judge, to become enthused or to become angry. No matter what we do about our anger, it always blocks us from taking action in a way that will heal and strengthen any situation. Dependent people seldom are able to avoid self-judgment and anger and cannot avoid increasing negative emotions. The deeper they fall into negative emotions, the harder it is to get back to choice.

We are in a world filled with substances that many use initially to escape their frustrations only to find that they have become dependent on them and have lost their ability to choose their path. They become more frustrated and more lost in the dilemma.

How do we help others work themselves free of their dependency? Where can we begin to get another's attention? Many people tell us that we must begin by helping the others understand that they are dependent. I submit to you that they already know that and this knowledge, by itself, is not enough. I believe that they only pay serious attention to the fact that they are dependent when the time comes to decide whether or not they are willing to die from it. Do you know what I mean? The issue is not that they are failing to see what they are doing, but that they are failing to see the consequences of what they are doing.

We live in a society filled with different opinions of what is right or wrong and what is good or bad. What one person thinks about the use of alcohol is all together different from another person who has been raised in a different culture or has been taught different religious doctrines. If you will step back and examine this issue, you will discover that we only choose to deal with a situation when we finally determine whether that experience is good or bad for us. Only then do we decide what we will do to correct or complete the situation.

It's rather interesting to watch people punish themselves. We all are capable of destroying ourselves, and it is only when we forgive ourselves that we can stop punishing ourselves. With some people, this is an intellectual decision while with others, it is an emotional decision. No matter how we make the ultimate decision, we will make it at the time we know we must make it. I don't care what the drug of choice or other situation is. We can overcome it through our power to choose. The power to choose is very powerful if we will only apply it.

Many who become dependent may be hiding from something in their lives. I want you to consider someone you may know who has a dependency and tell me if you can determine what he or she is hiding from. See if you can determine what the core issue is that is driving that person to want to avoid looking at it. I am talking about adults and not children. I will talk about our children later. Think about those who are lost behind any substance that blurs them from dealing with their challenges. These people have one thing in common. They are not willing to face their challenges.

Our role is to assist them in focusing on the challenge and in helping them understand that they have choices to make which, when made, can change the situation. If we are in a personal or business relationship with someone dealing with dependency, we can approach the issue with a clear and powerful message. This message is that they will eventually lose their lives if they continue down the path they are following. As strange as this statement sounds, stating this truth at the appropriate time is the only way to get the dependent person's attention. It is only a matter of time until any drug destroys the person's system to the point it collapses. That is the reality of using drugs. Once an individual takes responsibility for his or her life, we can then support that person in moving forward to deal with the underlying issues at hand.

We know that drugs are addictive. We also know that sometimes the drug takes years to kill us. What we do not always remember is that the longer we use a drug, the faster we weaken our ability to control it. It becomes progressive and cumulative. That is the reality of using drugs. The question remains, how to capture another person's attention? Since we are talking about adults, how would we talk to them about their dependency? Where would we start?

I have found three steps that work. However, we must make sure that we take each step in total faith so that it will open the door to help the others make their ultimate decision. It may take you several attempts to achieve your breakthrough to the other person, but the goal is to achieve it so we must remember the goal and not give up on it.

The three steps to take are: (1) Let the other person know that we are willing to accept their behavior; (2) Tell them we are willing to support them in eliminating the dependency; and (3) Tell them they have choice as to whether or not they will end their life this way. I know this sounds rather severe but it is the only way to get the dependent person's attention. When he or she has responded to our statements, we can then determine what our next step will be.

Normally, the next step will lead into three options: (1) Ask them to make an agreement with you regarding what they are going to do with the dependency;(2) Take them by the hand to a clinic that can provide professional support in clearing the control of the drug; and (3) Guide them to obtain professional assistance.

Once you have been able to gain the other person's confidence to move forward and walk with you to develop a plan to eliminate their challenge, you will find renewed peace and increased intimacy in your relationship. Always reinforce that you love them and trust them as they move forward. Also, demonstrate that you accept them in each stage of their recovery.

When we look at our children and their environment, we see how many of them can become hooked on drugs because of peer pressure or simply the need to be accepted by their group. Many parents have been faced with these challenges and have failed to help their children because they failed to get their child's attention until it was too late for the child to be able to control the situation without professional intervention.

There are so many case studies discussing dependency. Instead of reviewing case studies, I want to share with you how I view the dilemma and where I see we can best support our children. As children reach the age when they normally are most susceptible to experimentation with drugs, they are also at the age when they want to start making more and more of their own decisions. It is our responsibility to teach them to be effective decision-makers and to guide them as to what their reference points should be in making their own decisions.

The best way to guide our children is to teach them to be responsible decision-makers and to further teach them the importance of the agreements they make with self and others. So, when dealing with the subject of drugs, at any point of their experience, the most effective way to guide our children is through working with them to establish clear agreements. In other words, teach them to manage themselves and their relationship with others by honoring their agreements.

In order for our children to be able to make agreements with anyone, they must demonstrate that they are able to make clear choices without anyone or anything blocking them. It is at this point where you can get their attention regarding drugs. What you can say to them is simply that drugs have been created to help people escape reality and if one only used them under the guidance of a physician, a few drugs would have some value. However, several drugs have become a part of many people's social life and different people have different patterns for addiction. This confuses children as to why and when to use alcohol.

Many parties are organized around using alcohol or cocaine or one of the new synthetic drugs that have been created to generate a number of different experiences. So, the best option is simply to avoid using drugs altogether.

When using any drug, it will inhibit the user's ability to choose the best options, which can lead to unwanted or undesirable experiences. It is not necessary to preach to them about all of the bad experiences. It is also not necessary to threaten or berate your children at any point in your attempt to support them. What is necessary is to continuously remind them that the one option they have to become independent adults is their power of choice and that drugs destroy this power. At any time, you can also use this issue as a way to help them make agreements with you and teach them how important it is to keep their agreements.

I ask you to consider also how much the issue of keeping agreements has to do with the element of trust. Children need to be taught at a very young age how important trust is in all relationships. If you will show them the value of trust, they will be able to understand why this is more important to them than going along with suggestions from peers or simply believing that one experiment with a drug will not harm them. It is not that any one experience harms us. It is more important to understand that we all become creatures of habit and we cannot predict when dependency will arrive.

I don't know how many times a person will require taking any drug for it to become addictive. I only know that everyone will become addicted in time and the addition will lead to poor decision-making. It will also lead to lack of self-control and eventual physical and emotional deterioration. Have an honest conversation with your children and approach the subject of drugs from the point of view I have just shared with you and see how they respond.

We realize how important it is for you and I to be an effective guide to our children. I use the word "effective" because we need to effect a positive change in their lives. We want to be able to prepare them to live their lives as responsible and productive adults. We also want to guide them to become strong adults with productive careers and peaceful relationships. And most importantly, we want them to know God on a personal basis and understand the value and importance of His laws. Could it be that we can be better guides than we currently are?

Maybe I have not been the best parent in the past, but I do know one important thing for sure, which is that I have given my children a picture of how life works. I have taught them that regardless of the turmoil or the temptations around them, they do have choice and through this powerful gift, they can remove themselves from many challenges and escape many disasters in both their personal and business lives.

I have had several discussions with parents who have experienced one of their children becoming addicted to a drug. They have often felt that they were in some way responsible for their son's or daughter's behavior. Rarely is that true. Most of the time, they simply did not know how to handle the situation and became caught up in the turmoil. Most of the time, these people could not get the child's attention because they had either waited to long to take action or simply failed to be able to relate to the child. Most of these people have not been able to find peace until they at least reached the child and achieved getting their attention.

When we are dealing with any situation where drugs are creating turmoil, then we must become involved and get the right message to these young people. I have a client who has a teenage son who was coming home with alcohol on his breath but would not admit what was going on. Carl and I talked about his situation and what he could do to get his son to at least admit what he was doing. I suggested that he take a simple approach the next time his son came home with alcohol on his breath. My approach was to ask his son who was driving the car he was riding in during the evening. Then ask him who else was in the car with him. Once he shares that information, ask him if he is willing to call these friend's parents to let them know that they have been enjoying a few drinks during the evening. Ask him if he will call the driver's father first and let him also know that he can't ride with him anymore because he wants to enjoy life for as many years as possible. I told him to just ask those questions and nothing else and see what his son would say.

A few days later Carl noticed again that Don came home with alcohol on his breath. This time, instead of confronting Don to admit he had been drinking, he asked Don who was driving the car that evening and who all was with him. He didn't ask anything regarding where they had gone or who had purchased the alcohol. He just asked those questions and let Don go on to bed after he had answered them.

The next morning at breakfast, Carl asked Don the next set of questions. Needless to say, Don was not excited about the prospect of calling any of his friends' parents to make sure they knew about their escapades. He again denied that he or his friends had been drinking the night before. His father began to challenge his statements but then decided not to say anything more that day. We talked about his experience later that week and Carl concluded that the overall issue was fear of being discovered because Don already knew he was doing something that was not in his best interest.

Carl considered calling the other parents himself but we both realized he might end up positioning all of the boys against their parents if we took that approach. Carl told me he had not had any other experiences where Don had refused to tell him the truth. He could not understand why it was so important to deny what the boys were doing. We finally decided to take a very simple approach to the situation. The approach was to ask Don to make an agreement with him.

That evening, Carl asked Don to make an agreement with him. The agreement Don was asked to make was that he would not ride in any car when any alcohol was present nor would he ride with any driver who had been drinking. For a few minutes Don again tried to deny that anyone had been drinking but Carl simply came back to his basic request that Don would make this agreement with him. Finally, Don made the agreement with his father. Carl acknowledged him for making the agreement and further told him he had confidence Don would keep the agreement. He then told Don that if he discovered that Don had failed to keep the agreement, the consequences would be that he would not be allowed to obtain a driver's license or drive the car until he was of drinking age (which in our state is age 21). He now had now obtained Don's full attention.

It was at this point that Don asked Carl what the big deal was about drinking a few beers. Don said that everyone he knows has a beer from time to time and he often comes home from school to see Carl enjoying a drink or two. His question was why the big deal for him and his friends? All this time, Don had refused to take the subject seriously although he had already been told in school the dangers of drinking and driving. But he had not taken personal responsibility for his decisions.

Don respected his father and would not deliberately defy him. So, now Don would have to face up to the issue and decide for himself whether or not he would lie again and break this agreement. He was now facing the reality that he was being held accountable for his actions. Facing it, his current thinking about the whole subject had finally spilled out into their conversation.

How many times has the attitude of "what's the big deal" gotten children into serious trouble? How many young people have had their lives cut short by being in the wrong car at that wrong time? The only way to reduce this possibility is to help our children understand that they do have the power of choice and that you hold them accountable for their choices. The more you can reinforce to them how important their word is to you, the more you will help them build a life filled with taking their word and their agreements seriously.

Carl set his posture with Don who made an agreement which he kept. Whatever pattern was developing was broken as Don chose not to participate in his friend's weekly experiment with alcohol. Carl has no idea what they all talked about or how they decided to stop the pattern of activity they had started. He only knew that Don decided not to take the issue lightly and should be better prepared to examine his own use of alcohol as he grows older. Perhaps Carl can now start preparing Don to make a decision regarding the use of alcohol before he goes to college.

It's so important to teach children the importance of remaining in full control of their decision-making ability at all times. Children are not dumb nor are they, in most cases, deliberately trying to defy us. They are simply making decisions without understanding the consequences of these decisions. Drugs are easy to find. They are often pleasant to experience and are certainly a part of many groups' social events. Often, they are found in our home and children learn from us how to use them and why we use them. We are being short-sighted if we fail to realize how we are affecting our children by our own use of alcohol.

So, I wanted to talk about this issue because it affects so many people and their families. We are living in an age when more and more people are attempting to escape life's challenges through the temporary escape they believe drugs can provide. We are also living in an age when we have an increasing number of people with challenges and frustration in their lives. We have been taking a look at different issues which are causing turmoil in our society, and this subject is one of great importance to examine when considering what we can do to turn things around.

I wanted to share these issues with you as it saddens me when I see people dealing with fear and unable to make their own decisions due to some form of dependency that they have allowed to creep into their lives.

I must close now and get some exercise. I hope you and Ted are making progress through your talks. Do no hesitate to let me know if I can be of any additional support.

Your friend always,

James

XVIII

Is There a Way to Achieve the Perfect Divorce?

"Principles for Completing Marriages in Peace and Love"

Dear Gloria:

It was so good to hear from you. I look forward to seeing you again when you are in Southern California next month, so call us when you have finalized your schedule. I am sorry to hear that your brother Jerry and his wife have decided to separate. From what you outlined in your letter, I can understand their situation as well as their concerns as to how the divorce will affect their children. Divorce is often a time of turmoil, but there are principles and steps that can make it far more positive. I am going to share them with you in the hope you will be able to share them with both Jerry and Helen and apply them yourself should you and Ted choose to take that path in your relationship.

I am fascinated when I watch people deal with completing a marriage because they always have to deal with their feelings and emotions. Seldom have I seen a divorce that didn't revolve around who was right and who was wrong or some very hurt feelings. As we have seen in other situations, there are numerous events that trigger the turmoil, and each person will react differently as the relationship evolves toward the final separation. It is often difficult for the couple to focus on or agree to the core issues which are always evident long before the final phase of their relationship. So, they often get lost in their negative emotions when they should be focused on creating a new relationship especially when young children are involved.

What I have learned is that this is a time for both partners to focus on applying the principles of highest truth and highest purpose and choosing to take the necessary steps to allow these principles to heal their situation. In reality, the relationship no longer meets their needs and therefore must be completed. Although this will bring up feelings of guilt and failure, finding highest purpose will always help each one accept the situation. In addition, highest truth will always set them free and highest love will heal every feeling and emotion.

Your brother is a good man and I have always seen Helen as a kind and responsible person. I am glad to hear that they are both good parents. Since they were married in their 20's, both of them have had a dozen years to begin discovering who they really are and what they want from life. You have pointed out that they are opposites; what used to look like balance has now emerged to create frustration and antagonism, as each one looks at the other's point of view and how he or she acts or reacts to each situation. Although people with opposite personalities can always learn something from each other's traits and social style, they often find that they do not build long-term friendships as they simply don't accept the other person's behavior.

I have also found that the harder the two people work to compromise or try to ignore their issues, the faster emotional separation can set in. The more they struggle to change each other, the faster antagonism, anger and resentment emerge. So, I can understand how Jerry and Helen feel and that Jerry now wants to complete the relationship but Helen wants them to start over and feels they both can change.

Regardless of what has happened between them, both Jerry and Helen realize their marriage was not made in heaven. As you have pointed out, they also realize that they have been struggling with the relationship for several months and have not been demonstrating to their children what a solid marriage is all about. Whether they realize it or not, their children already are feeling insecure and urgently need for them to demonstrate how to maintain love and peace within the family. I like to think that they will now want to create a new relationship through the divorce that will help each child feel secure and loved.

When I look at the foundation of marriage, it is a trust-based relationship based on agreements between two people. Both partners must determine and communicate their individual wants and needs and then they should establish mutual goals and objectives. Marriage requires a level of commitment in that each partner pledges to meet the other partner's needs. To work and grow, a marriage also requires ongoing acceptance and intimacy. Without acceptance and intimacy, it will die. Regardless of what each of the spouses has been taught by their parents about the role they should play in their marriage, they must eventually adapt a role that meets their wants and needs. As we grow, we discover that our wants and needs change just as children's wants and needs change as they grow through childhood and adolescence.

It appears that Jerry and Helen have reached the point where they have changed so much they now find it difficult if not impossible to meet each other's needs. They now need to negotiate new agreements so that they can grow in new directions and meet their children's needs. This is where their transition can be quite challenging unless they make their decisions in highest purpose, truth and love. These principles hold the key to success in this situation.

Both Jerry and Helen must see the value and be willing to exchange the relationship that is not working with one that will work. This is achieved through facing the situation and reaching new agreements—agreements that will change their roles, support their children and allow each other to meet their wants and needs.

In many cases, one of the partners arrives at the conclusion that the relationship must be changed before the other one is willing to accept the other's point of view. This often creates negative emotions that will affect the couple's children if not corrected. The reality is that antagonism arises when one partner does not live up to the expectations of the other partner. In Jerry's case, he is not living up to Helen's expectations because she has yet to accept his point of view concerning divorce.

What Jerry needs to communicate now is that he still has love for Helen and wants both of them to focus on the one area that is working in their relationship, which is their relationship with the children. That is the one area where they can create new roles, set new goals and objectives, and demonstrate love and acceptance. Simply stated, they must let the children know immediately that they are not losing their parents. They must also let the children know that they are secure and that the transition will not affect their security.

Finally, they must reinforce in each child that they love each other as parents and that they love the children. Maintaining love toward the children will start the healing process and help establish a new relationship with new elements of acceptance and cooperation. As I have already shared, the principle of highest love will heal and strengthen during a time when both parties can be dealing with resentment and guilt.

As the process of divorce begins, there are often feelings of failure and isolation. You can support Jerry and Helen by letting them know that they are not going to be excluded from your social events just because they are separating. This is an issue that can affect one or both parties if they have built friendships over the years with other couples. This situation is further complicated when both couples have children who've formed close friendships. Jerry and Helen should each be able to continue their relationship with you and others in your family. Their children should be able to come and see you frequently without Jerry and Helen needing to be there together.

The principle of highest purpose can help frame every new agreement they make around how to maintain the strongest level of consistency for the children while they organize their long-term plans and deal with new living arrangements.

Another area that can create real turmoil is when there is another person involved. Since Jerry has already met someone else, he would be wise to keep her out of the conversations with Helen. Hopefully, he can help Helen realize that the other woman is not the problem but simply a product of their failure to hold each other in their hearts. I do understand that infidelity is a serious breach in any marriage but since this is not the case, Jerry should not feel guilty about his new relationship.

I am always sad when I learn that one of the partners is attempting to maintain two relationships at the same time. Regardless of their situation, this approach never works and always ends up creating more turmoil. So, here is another case where the truth will set us free. When someone needs and wants another person other than his or her spouse, they would be wise to take a very close look at themselves and why they are involved with the new person. We can make a divorce a much smoother experience if we will complete the first relationship before getting too involved in the second one.

Jerry and Helen need to complete some serious financial planning now. This is a time when they should focus on protecting their assets and dealing objectively with support and childcare agreements. Too often, couples fight over money and try to punish each other by arguing about support and child care. My solution is to apply a very simple principle to financial planning during a divorce, which is to do unto others as you would have them do unto you. When applied, this principle will always bring things into proper perspective no matter how much it hurts or how angry one is in the moment.

One last area that creates turmoil in a divorce is arguments concerning custody of the children. Unless one of the parents is dealing with issues which clearly would require that they would not be able to provide responsible custody, this area must always be one where the custody is shared. We can feel very strongly about other person's inadequacies during the early stages of a divorce. However, my experience is that both parents need to continue to be involved in order for the children to learn how to maintain respect for each parent. Respect is an important element of friendship and we are always wise to take every possible step to rebuild the friendship as estranged spouses so that our children can see and benefit from this important element within every long-term relationship. Both parents should remember that no matter what they choose to do in their personal lives, they will be parents for the rest of their lives.

We never should meddle in another's life nor is it wise to offer advice which is not requested. But you can ask Jerry if there is any way you can support him and if he has anyone to support him with his decision-making at this time. This can be a good time to ask him if this is the time for him to choose to be in highest purpose, truth and love. Choosing and applying these principles is the only way to complete a marriage in peace and love.

We are leaving today for Newport Beach and hope we have our normal good weather as I am looking forward to a long walk on the beach. My thoughts will be with you and Ted this weekend. Please give Ted our best regards and let him know we also value his friendship. I am forever grateful that we have peace and joy in highest purpose and that love always strengthens us if we will only choose to accept our situations. Until we talk again, I wish you peace and love.

Your friend always,

James

SECTION FOUR

Managing Your Career Transition

XIX

Can We Take Control of Our Career?

"How to Re-Evaluate Where Your Job Security Lies"

Dear Teresa:

I trust my letter finds you well and prospering. It was great hearing from you and getting an update on what's going on in your life. Please give Harry my best regards. We have all been very busy planning for the coming New Year as well as preparing for the holiday season. I trust that you and your family will have a very Happy Holiday and of course a Happy New Year. In response to your questions in your letter, I want to share some thoughts regarding how we can take greater control of our careers by continually looking for new opportunities.

Planning always affords us the time to re-evaluate our career and explore where new opportunities exist for us. It is a great time to take a serious and objective look at what is really going on in our company, our industry and new areas for improving and expanding our products and services. It also presents an opportunity to evaluate ourselves and how we can best prepare to meet these new opportunities.

Several years ago, my wife and I attended a meeting chaired by the head of the MBA department of one of our universities here in California. The topic of discussion was the university's perceived failure of their MBA program to adequately prepare the students to enter the business world. The department head ended the group discussion by concluding that the most important elements for success were when the element of preparation met the element of opportunity. We should always remember this hypothesis as it makes so much practical sense.

We have a growing number of clients considering a change in careers due to layoffs and burnout. I remember the first time I experienced so many people around me dealing with career change. It was back in the late 1980's and early 1990's, when the layoffs began in the aerospace industry in Southern California. Within a period of eighteen months, thousands of men and women were on the street without the job that had framed their very image of self. The experience of preparing resumes and trying to get back into an industry that would probably never hire them again took its toll on so many of them, both emotionally and financially. People were literally hanging out at various employment agencies much like crowds hung around the soup kitchens during the Great Depression.

They were living in one of the most dynamic economic regions in the world but now were unemployed. Prior to the rapid events which preceded the layoffs, I had read numerous glowing reports about how many new jobs would be created in Southern California, and how robust its economy was. These reports positioned the Los Angeles area as one of the fastest growing regions for economic growth in the United States. Yet, I personally witnessed an economy that played havoc with the lives of thousands of people who had the experience and credentials that had placed them in positions that enabled them to live the good life for a large segment of their adult lives. I will talk more about this experience later.

I want to tell you another story about a client who has made a successful career transition. I know you can relate to this story and hopefully remember it if you are ever arrive at the time when you are ever faced with making this decision. I will share with you Julie's experience. When Julie first asked to meet with me, she was Director of Human Resources for one of the fortune 500 companies operating in the Bay Area. She was taking home over $150,000 each year in salary and benefits. However, Julie was burned out and tired of all of the pressure associated with her position and the politics of her work environment. Several of her friends had resigned from her company and had taken positions in a new start-up, where they were excitedly anticipating their future.

Julie was thinking about joining their new company and was seeking our support for making her decision. Her primary challenge was that although she would be granted an attractive package of stock options, she would have to take a reduction in salary of about $50,000 per year, which of course would dramatically affect her cash flow. Julie was a single parent and was concerned that she would not be able to survive her transition without negatively affecting her thirteen-year-old daughter Amanda.

Julie said that she had thought about becoming a consultant in the past but felt she was not prepared. So, she had not taken any serious steps to investigate how she could make that transition. My friend Julie was now caught up in the excitement she could feel from talking with her friends about the new company. It didn't seem to be important to any of them that the new company lacked a product, or that it might be two or three years before the company would have any revenues. What was important to all of her friends was that the environment was light-years better than their old company and of course they all had a new sense of hope for the future. Since many of her friends were engineers, they were busy focusing on research and development of the new company's technology. They knew they would be busy and challenged for the next few years.

Julie had enrolled in our Transition Planning Program to prepare herself for her transition. One day, I had the opportunity to sit in on one of Julie's transition planning meetings for a few minutes. We had just completed a discussion concerning her financial and tax planning for the year, during which she told me she had a couple of issues that needed to be resolved regarding her transition. I wanted to hear what she would say to my associate during their meeting so I asked if I could sit in on one of their sessions.

When I joined them, they were talking about the issue of assurances and guarantees. You know that's a subject that always seems to come up when looking at anything new. What guarantees were there that the new company would ever be able to get its product to market? How sure was she that the new company had the capital to sustain the company considering its lack of revenue? What assurances did she have that the stock options and stock bonuses would ever be worth anything?

After about five minutes of listening to their conversation, I asked Julie if I could interject a question. My question was, in thinking about what she really wanted to do with her career, had she considered where her passion lay? I asked her where she thought she could make the greatest contribution. Julie thought for a moment about my question and then made an honest comment. She said, "If I had the money, I would start my own consulting business. If only I could get someone to invest in me I wouldn't work for any company anymore because I am now prepared to operate a consulting business and I feel there is a great opportunity now."

For the first time in our conversation that day, I heard the words "if only, I'm prepared, and great opportunity." Julie was selling out her dream because she did not see how she could survive financially if she started her own consulting business. She felt that her security was in having cash on hand to ensure that she could pay her bills. When in reality, her security was in her talents and skills, her present preparation, and the current opportunity in her industry. Julie was placing her sense of security in the wrong place and this was limiting her ability to make a decision that was so important to her emotional, intellectual and financial life.

After Julie made her statement, my response was, "Julie, I like your prospects for building a financially secure consulting business better than the prospects of the new startup you have been thinking about joining. I recommend that you consider developing your personal business plan and I am confident you will find a way to finance your transition if you really want to become a consultant."

At that point, Julie made one of the most important decisions of her life. Her decision was to invest her energy and her future in herself. From that moment on, there was never another word spoken about joining the new startup. She obtained the necessary financing to make her transition from her aunt and established her own consulting business. Her business has thrived as more and more companies outsource their human resource services to independent consultants instead of setting up their own human resource department. This was a decision which has proven to be most valuable to Julie.

Over the years, I have been a part of several successful business ventures. Many of my clients have been in business for years and continue to earn a consistent level of income necessary to maintain the lifestyle they have established for themselves and their families. During my experience in working with these successful business owners, I have discovered that they all have something in common. What they have in common is that they know that they do not have to count on any company to take care of them. Their security is in their talents and skills, and in their freedom to make their own choices.

In my next letter, I am going to share several other success stories about people I have worked with who've made rewarding career transitions. This is a good time in our lives to remember that no one is born to be a slave to any business. We need not stay in an industry which lacks opportunity just because that is what we have always done. No one comes into this world designated to get lost in the corporate jungle, or predestined to become a business failure.

Sometimes we cannot see our way clear of our challenges and sometimes we take the wrong steps. Yet we know that we have principles we can apply to help us gain control of our lives and build security for ourselves and our family. Remembering that we have the greatest probability for success when preparation meets opportunity is one of the most important principles for managing our career.

I must close this letter as we are preparing for Thanksgiving Dinner. I have a deep feeling of thankfulness and abundance this year and hope that you feel the same. I always enjoy hearing from you and I am happy that you are prospering and happy. I will write again soon.

Your friend always,

James

CAN WE CONQUER THE CHALLENGES OF CAREER TRANSITION?

"Principles to Support You During Your Career Transition"

Dear Teresa:

It was great to hear from you again. I am glad you are enjoying good health and are prospering. I'm also happy to learn that you enjoyed my last letter and understand your thoughts concerning preparing ourselves as we look for growth opportunities. We are taking time now to prepare for a major transition in our company. I am sure it will bring us new challenges as well as new rewards. As we move ahead, I will continue to apply the principles I have learned to rely on every time I am faced with a new challenge.

It is always rewarding as we observe how the principles support us in achieving our breakthroughs. Many people apply them once and, when they do not see immediate results, they discard them. All of the principles are like seeds that we plant. The more we apply them, the more they grow. The more they grow, the stronger they become. So, have confidence and faith in the principles and focus on the results you wish to achieve.

In this letter, I want to examine the phenomenon of corporate lay-offs and how lay-offs create turmoil in so many people's lives. This is emerging as a cause for escalating feelings of doubt and insecurity for many people in their 40's and 50's. It has also affected a number of our clients in their early 60's who would like to continue working for at least ten years. It is a reality of corporate life that companies will lay off people during times when their profits are down. In addition, there are cycles of mergers and acquisitions that often affect the employees who work for the acquired as well as the surviving company. Add to these events the reality that many people are reexamining where they will direct their career in the future and we find that a larger percentage of our population now finds themselves in some turmoil. Career transition can be a challenging experience and is the topic we should continue to explore so we can best support those around us.

I have recently spoken with several clients recently who are currently struggling to find some honest answers to perplexing questions about the future of their careers. Add this to the experience of discovering that they are on their company's early retirement list, and now they must begin the process of dealing with all of the unknowns they will face in the future.

It's been ten years since the aerospace industry began laying off people by the thousands, forcing them to deal with the unknown. More importantly, the layoffs forced many to realize that they would never find employment again, within the parameters they had grown to understand and trust as their sphere of career opportunity. Those people were dealing with many of the same challenges our friends and neighbors are dealing with today. They also lived in affluent communities throughout the United States where large and historically solid companies had provided them with economic and career security. They had access to many of the same resources available today, for investigating their alternatives, but few of them made it through the experience without learning some valuable lessons.

One lesson learned by many people during that period was that there was no one who could give them the assurances and guarantees they were looking for. No one could provide simple answers or make it easy for them to make financial and career decisions, or choose new directions.

When the layoffs and offers to take early retirement started, we began receiving calls from people seeking information and introductions for new employment opportunities. I can tell you it was a time of frustration and financial struggle for many who had been enjoying the good life for quite some time. Many were forced to sell homes they had lived in for years in order to free up the funds to meet financial obligations, and compelled to shift their career in a totally new direction. It was also a time when many found that they had far fewer options for maintaining the same income they were enjoying before their termination.

I remember several people who had been in management positions prior to their layoff discovering that they would have to take positions with smaller companies with limited resources in order to remain in a management position. Worse yet, they found that the pay and benefits were dramatically lower than what they were accustomed to. For many, new salaries where far less than their standard of living demanded, and they struggled with how this affected their own quality of life, as well as the quality of lifestyles their family had come to enjoy. Others discovered after a short period of time that they were not suited for the new environment, while some found the work boring and unchallenging.

I remember working with an executive, Vaughn, who was struggling with how his transition was affecting his standard of living. He was also struggling to make an intelligent decision about his vocational future. He was in his early 50's, and had served as the manager of the accounting department for one of the aerospace giants. His wife had invested the last five years raising their three younger children and felt it was important to continue in her present role. They owned a nice house atop a hill affording a magnificent view of San Diego's harbor. They both loved their neighborhood and dreaded the thought of moving to a new community, if Vaughn was forced to seek employment out of the area.

The key question in Vaughn's mind was how to maintain his family's present lifestyle while dealing with the reality that he needed to architect a change in his career. He had the option of moving to Singapore where his company operated a subsidiary. He also had the option of taking a position at a local bank, at half the salary he had been earning. For several weeks Vaughn looked at other job alternatives and wrestled with the possibility that he would need to move his family to another area of the country to solve his challenge.

One day, as we waited for our breakfast order to be taken, I asked Vaughn to if he would be interested in examining the possibility of buying and operating a business. He said he had thought about that idea the previous evening but could not see how he could finance such a transition. He reminded me that he only had about $25,000 left in his savings and taking money from his retirement fund would be too expensive considering the related taxes and penalties that would be incurred as the result of withdrawing money from that account.

Vaughn and I discussed the type of business he would like to own and how he saw himself working in the business. He left our luncheon meeting with a new spirit of excitement and promised he would get back to me within a few days to continue our conversations. Later that day I talked with a couple of franchisors and located two existing franchises for sale in his area which I thought might be of interest to him. Sometimes the franchisors know about franchisees, who for one reason or another, would like to sell their business and can be of assistance in a number of valuable ways.

Anyway, we were moving forward and at our next meeting I reviewed my ideas with Vaughn about buying a franchise. He was now very much interested in exploring the possibility of becoming a business owner. However, his primary challenge was where to get the $150,000 he would need to acquire the business. I remember saying to him that this was a time to determine what was most important to him. Why not take the time to list, in order of importance, what he wanted for himself and his family.

Vaughn accepted my recommendation and completed his list while we were waiting for breakfast to be served. The first item on his list was to make sure that his wife and children were least affected by the career decision. The next item of importance was to be able to remain in the same community. After that he decided the next priority was to determine what he would be doing in his career for the next five years, as that was the time horizon he had established for this phase of his career. Then came earning enough from his new career to maintain the quality of life he and his family now enjoyed. The last goal was to remain close to their church which was important to both Vaughn and his wife.

After we finished breakfast, I told Vaughn he had just answered the question concerning where he would get the money. I pointed out that the money was in the $250,000 of equity in his present home. Why not sell it and invest the $150,000 in his future and take the remaining $100,000 and buy another house in a newer development not that far from his present home. His children would be able to go to the same schools and they would be able to attend their church without any challenges whatsoever.

Vaughn looked at me and almost cried as he realized that he had solved his challenge simply by prioritizing the most important issues in his life. He followed through with his plan and today, ten years later, he remains happy and prospering in his new career.

Looking back on my first major experience in working with people going through career transitions, I also remember that a number of those we met with were struggling with their image of self. They felt they were not needed or wanted as they tried to process the shock that they had just been terminated. After years of leading a team or functioning as the lead project engineer, they were now attempting to locate any job, even if it required that they would have to move hundreds or thousands of miles from the community where they had developed their roots.

I also remember people spending most of their time going on one job interview after another. Others spent hours posting their resume at numerous places. Few that I talked with took the time to determine exactly where new opportunities existed. I also realize that many of the challenges these professionals faced in the 1980's were the same ones being faced today by thousands of people.

Fortunately, there are some fundamental steps that can be taken to reduce the negative impact from the experience. Let's start our analysis by acknowledging that many educated people will immediately turn to research in an attempt to determine what their options are. Their challenge is that there is so much information available. I have found that one can become frozen in analysis and not be able to develop a plan. So, the first fundamental to learn from these people's past experience is that we should determine what our overall needs and goals are before shifting to a research mode. This requires discussions with people who have the skills to assist us in asking the right questions, instead of telling us what they would do, or what they feel we should do.

I had an interesting experience with Doris who, after a year of being unemployed, came in to talk with one of our transition planners. She said that she was absolutely drained from looking at dozens of career options and that she was very confused and concerned about her future. At 43, she had ample time to find a new direction, but couldn't determine which industry to pursue because her research had determined that all of the ones she had researched were having challenges during the particular recession. I met her during her second meeting with one of our advisors. She told me that day that she was considering moving to Kansas were she could live with her mother and continue her research. I asked her what she enjoyed doing and if she had any particular passions. She said she loved to read and could spend the rest of her life reading about history. I asked her if she had ever considered becoming a librarian. Immediately her face lit up. For the first time, she began looking at her transition with the end in mind. She would start contacting the colleges and public libraries to establish a career in that field.

Two months later, Doris had obtained a job in the library of one of the local schools and she continues to enjoy her new career to this day.

The second point to learn from this example is that exhaustive research seldom, if ever, provided the job-seekers with any assurances or guarantees regarding what could be achieved in the future. Several have told me that their research only left them more confused and frustrated. We have learned from them that we should first step back and determine where our passions lie, and what we can enthusiastically see ourselves doing for the next five years. Take some time to explore your dreams and passions, and then seek out the best opportunities to fulfill them.

As I see it, the people who made the smoothest transition were the ones who let go of trying to get all of the details of the many options they managed to uncover. They made better progress when they developed a short list of viable opportunities and then began the process of gathering and dissecting information. Further, in conducting research, we would be wise to speak with those who have "been there and done that"—instead of relying on the volumes of information available on the Internet, or taking advice from friends and relatives who feel they know best.

Another point to remember is that we must be willing to look at new alternatives for earning a living and, at the same time, to find a new career that can continue to feed us intellectually and emotionally. To achieve these goals, it is very important to look at what we truly enjoy doing, what our innate talents and skills are, and what stimulates us on both an emotional and intellectual level. Those we worked with who shifted their focus to what they would truly enjoy doing, and new possibilities for investment of time and money, achieved far greater results then those who tried to hold on to past images of what they should do for a living. Great progress was made in their new directions even when they had no previous experience or training. When needed, they obtained the necessary training very rapidly. Moreover, they found their new options intellectually stimulating and emotionally rewarding.

Before making any major decisions concerning your next job, or starting or buying a business or franchise it is wise to obtain some solid tax effective financial planning. This planning should incorporate a thorough analysis of how to utilize financing and passive assets like those in your 401k. It should also analyze the impact of tapping home equity or selling assets that may create substantial tax liabilities. Be sure to take time to examine what assets to use for your transition planning, and which ones to leave alone for future income.

In simplest terms, there are two primary sources of income to provide us and our families with the standard of living we desire. One is us at work; the second, our assets at work. The majority of people being laid off today have most of their assets in their 401k, or in their home equity. Financial planning is important to avoid spending assets that are currently set aside for long-term retirement income. It is important not to liquidate the wrong assets at the wrong time to make it through their transition. Current market conditions demand careful analysis of which assets should be liquidate and which assets borrowed against if borrowing is necessary.

Here is another important point to remember. After the layoffs, a number of the people who sold their primary residence and moving to an area where they could acquire cheaper housing have since told me that they feel they made the wrong decision. Although they were able to free up assets for income through the sale of their house, a large number became disenchanted with their new community and some lost contact with friends and relatives, an important element in their lives. So, before you place the "For Sale" sign on your lawn, obtain some solid counseling regarding this area of planning.

Through proper planning and timely professional support, many others have been able to achieve a major transition in a period of 12 to 18 months, and have successfully avoided the challenges that others have experienced with less adequate planning.

One final point to remember is that the people who focused on new options instead of the perceived problems made it through the experience much faster and with less short-term financial or emotional damage. They avoided running out of severance pay as they developed a new plan for their future shortly after their unemployment started. They discovered that embracing change with a new blueprint for their future raises the probability of future success. They learned to shift their focus from the negatives to looking for the positives and, in doing so, discovered new careers, new business opportunities and for some, new investment opportunities. Perhaps these discoveries would never have been achieved if they had continued to dwell on their situation with the same thoughts and feelings they had when they began the transition.

While there are many valuable lessons that can be learned from the past, there are also vital principles and active steps to take to achieve the needed changes a number of people now face. I must close now but will write again soon. As always, I trust you are at peace and continuing to enjoy your life.

Your friend always,

James

XXI

Can You Survive the Request to Take Early Retirement?

"How to Reinvent Your Career"

Dear Teresa:

I trust my letter finds you well and prospering. I am making progress in restructuring our business and now I am about ready to implement my plans for the future. It's been a good experience in creating and correcting. From your letter, it sounds as though you are making progress with your career planning. I have continued to focus on your questions and have a story I want to share with you highlighting what I learned from Bill and Sharon.

When I think about Bill and Sharon and their experience, I'm reminded again that what we choose to correct, complete or create controls what happens in the future. However, our first decision is to face up to the challenges and take steps to eliminate the situations in our lives that are blocking us from achieving our long-term plans for career transitions. And as I have shared with you before, applying these principles can support us in facing each situation.

When I first met Bill and Sharon, both worked for established companies in corporate America, and had done so for over ten years. Bill was 60 and Sharon was 40. This was a second marriage for both, and Bill's children were old enough that they did not need to factor them into their future career goals.

Although Sharon had been working full time for the past three years, she had taken some time off prior to meeting Bill to invest more time with her two children who were then nine and thirteen years old. Sharon was involved in marketing communications and was a relationship manager with her company's fifty largest clients.

Bill was a project manager at one of the big electronic firms in our area. He was struggling to keep things going smoothly within a division that basically was going to be phased out in the near future due to changes in technology. Within two or three years at the most, the area of technology in which Bill had received all of this training and experience would be dead. In just two to three years, Bill would be faced with making a serious career decision.

Bill was smart enough to see that he had no place to go—and also recognized that no company would pay him what he had been earning to retrain him for a short career in another field. Unless he came up with an option, Bill would be confronted with early retirement and he really did not want to face the possibility of having no where to go and nothing to do at that age. Bill's father was still in excellent health and very active at 85, and Bill worried about his future considering he had an excellent chance of living another 25 years or more.

Bill and I decided to approach their situation by developing a financial plan for their future, so that Sharon and the younger children would be secure regardless of what Bill chose to do. Although Sharon's ex-husband was contributing financially to their children and was still very involved in their lives, Bill wanted to make sure he too could contribute by being a good guide to the children. He hoped he could contribute by helping them to understand how important it was to discover and pursue what they each enjoyed doing, and that he could also contribute to their spiritual growth.

Together, we started our planning with the goal of examining each asset to determine what role it would play in the future. We figured into our analysis that Bill would find something to do that would generate at least 60% of what he was currently earning for another ten years and then factored in another 35% of his current earnings for an additional five years. Bill felt strongly that he should stay active in some level of work throughout his seventies, and knew that we all live longer when we have purpose in our lives and things to keep us mentally active.

It was during our second planning session that we discovered what Bill would do. This came while we were looking at the best strategy for the management of a rental property they owned. Although the rental continued to increase in value and had already appreciated to produce over $275,000 in net equity, it was not generating any measurable income because Bill had refinanced the mortgage several times to generate cash to help pay for two of his children's college expenses. We calculated that, at the best, he would only be able to project about $800 per month of positive income in three years from this investment which wasn't going to solve his income needs, or maximize a return on this investment.

I asked Bill if he and Sharon would consider selling the rental and investing the equity in a small business that Bill could use as his vehicle for his career, after his present department died. To this end, Bill agreed to meet with our business brokerage advisor to explore this possibility. Since Bill had never looked at the option of owning his own business, he had absolutely no idea of what kind of business he would enjoy owning. I recommended that he look first at his own skills and talents, and what he had naturally been successful doing in a corporate environment. Bill would be able to eliminate many options, and focus on fewer alternatives if he would first look at what he would enjoy doing, and how he wanted to be involved in this business.

After two weeks of serious thought, Bill called me rather excited to tell me what his answer was. He wanted to pursue a dream and interest he had discovered years ago, which was to become involved in the restaurant business. First, he wanted to own a restaurant catering to people who enjoyed seafood. Second, he wanted to develop different entrees and integrate his recipes within a Mexican food theme. Putting the two together, he wanted to own and operate a Mexican restaurant that specialized in exotic seafood dishes.

I was absolutely amazed at how enthusiastic Bill was about his idea. He had never mentioned his love for cooking, or his hidden passion. Now we were talking about Bill pursuing a new career, light years different from what he was currently doing in his career. It was very obvious that Bill had reached the top of the hill with his struggle to determine where he would point his career, and was now ready to sit down and create a plan for the future.

Within two months from the time we had our phone conversation about Bill's dream, we had located a restaurant for sale that would provide the base from which Bill could create his concept. Bill was also busy studying his new craft and creating recipes that would, in the future, rank his little restaurant as one of the top rated restaurants in his specialty.

So you see, Bill didn't wait for the axe to fall in his company. He sold his rental property and created a new career by investing the funds in the restaurant. Within a year from the date, he completed one phase of his life, and created a new one for himself and his family. When he approached his boss about the future of his division and offered to take an early retirement package, he was rewarded for his offer to step forward and reduce cost in that division through an attractive early retirement package. These funds provided Bill with the cash reserves to cover his share of the family budget while he was getting the business started.

Bill and Sharon have never been happier. Their sixteen year old son Ron is now working part-time at the restaurant and Bill is absolutely thrilled at the opportunity to use this time to guide Ron to examine how life works and where he can make a contribution. They are planning to take two vacations each year to visit restaurants in other countries and around the United States to get ideas to enhance the quality of their restaurant. I suspect they will be taking these trips and coming up with new recipes for years to come.

I salute Bill for achieving something few people permit themselves to dream or to achieve. He was able to reconnect with what he knew could make him happy and ignite his interest. He was able to shift his life in an entirely new direction by taking his eyes off the challenge and what he didn't want to happen, and shifting his focus onto seeing himself in a new role in his future that met his wants and needs.

So you see that before we can change anything, we must be able to determine where we want to go, and be able to have a clear picture of what our life will look like when we get there. Only then can we start down the path to complete business relationships that are not working for ourselves—and create new ones that will assist us in having a meaningful career we can control throughout the remainder of our lives.

As for me and my own personal planning, here is what I have decided. I choose to live my life as though my career is my preparation for eternal life. I want to be able to work with people forever, to be able to create, organize, and launch blueprints that will assist others to achieve financial freedom and take control over their lives. I plan to create programs in our company that will provide people with the principles and the action steps necessary to overcome adversity and build strength. And, I envision my associates reminding people for years to come that if they will apply the principles and steps we have been given, they will be able to live a life full of peace and prosperity.

I want to empower others through my actions, which requires that I take action and follow through to be a good example to those around me. I want the freedom that will allow me to spend my time and operate my business from California, the Virgin Islands or other places around the world I love to travel to. I want to develop processes that will assist my associates and clients in improving their effectiveness and productivity, and I choose to always be willing to change and grow.

I have shared these dreams with you for one reason. The reason is to share with you my methods for planning my future. We should not be forced to live the second half of our life with the probability that we can no longer be effective and productive in our careers. We have not obtained the education, gained the experience and expanded our minds, only to be told by someone else that we are not needed or wanted in the world of commerce just because we have a few specks of gray in our hair.

We cannot be faced with spending perhaps the greatest time of our lives looking at limited work opportunity or, worse yet, having nothing to do. We can correct the course of our career through conscious, creative choice. Through conscious creative choice, we can eliminate dead-end jobs and dead-end business relationships. We can all choose to change and create a new career direction for our future. It's all in our hands or, more specifically, in our hearts.

I am so happy you are focused on making a change, and I remain confident that you will take the steps necessary to achieve it. Change is difficult to achieve but not impossible. We must always know where we want to go so we can direct our path to get there.

I am going to close this letter now and take the time to look at some new opportunities I see emerging in our business. I trust you are also discovering new opportunities for your future. I look forward to hearing from you soon and trust you will have a great month.

Your friend always,

James

XXII

CAN YOUR CAREER SURVIVE
HEALTH CHALLENGES?

*"How to Ensure That Your Career Will Survive
Personal Illness"*

Dear Teresa:

I trust my letter finds you and your family well and prospering. We are all doing well and enjoying ourselves. I am delighted to hear about your progress in evaluating your career and hope that my thoughts have been helpful. I am writing to you today to share several new thoughts and the challenges of several of my other clients who are struggling with their careers. I trust these thoughts and stories will assist you in your evaluation of your future.

Yesterday, I went for a long walk to think about an area in my life that requires creating new options. My thoughts were on how to prepare myself for change. Where I live, we have several excellent trails we can walk along with a feeling that we are in the country, when in reality we are almost right in the middle of the town. One of the trails winds along a road and up a rather steep hill. The walk really gets your heart beating. As you reach the top of the hill, the path winds around a small lake where you can sit on one of many benches and relax before coming back down the hill.

As I started up the hill, I thought again about my discovery that there are three basic choices we have whenever we are faced with any situation that is drawing our unwanted attention. One option is to create a new alternative, the second option is to correct the existing situation, and the third is to simply complete or end the situation.

Now that you have arrived at the time in your life when you are examining career options, maybe you will decide to make a career change.

155

Regardless of what you decide to do, I want to support you in thinking through how to deal with all of the many issues that often stand in the way of making a clear decision. I appreciate your support when I have needed it and trust that I can be of assistance now. As you examine your future, you will find the three "C's" (correct, complete, and create) helpful.

I want to share with you some of the thoughts and concerns I had as I've personally been dealing with the future, and also tell you about the challenges and successes of two clients, Tom and Mary. Hopefully these stories will provide you with some insight to support you in creating a future that will not only meet your financial needs, but also provide you with the steps to take to achieve greater control of your career.

Today, I find myself right in the middle of a great career with many wonderful clients, plenty of work to do and ample opportunity to challenge me both intellectually and spiritually. But now it's time to plan for the next phase of my career. The present phase has taken about seven years to unfold, and has brought around me a number of people who have cont.ibuted so much to our present level of success. So, you may ask what my challenge is. The challenge is that it is now time to complete a plan that will dramatically change my functions during the next seven years. Actually, it is time to create a blueprint that will reshape everyone in our firm's functions during this period.

Unless we create our own blueprint for our future, we may find ourselves facing one of life's greatest challenges. This challenge is the lack of ongoing purpose or direction in our career. This can create potential frustration if our job is terminated and we don't know where to go or what to do. Yet, at any time in our lives, we still have the opportunity to create a new blueprint to build a new career filled with purpose and direction. We should do this planning with our spouses and work hard to understand each other's career needs and goals. We should also allocate in our blueprint more time for travel and relaxation as well as other activities we enjoy. Finally, we should be sure that we are both in agreement with each of the important milestones we will establish.

Our parents lived in an era when one worked to age 65 and then retired. Unless they owned their own business, they knew that was the basic plan. It was expected they would get out of the way and let the younger generation work. In the old days, some companies did provide a pension plan which set aside some money so they could "retire" with some financial security. As they entered that phase of their lives, their focus would then be controlled by whatever projects and interests they pursued with their free time. Lifespans were shorter then so fewer people were faced with years of idleness and lack of vocational fulfillment.

Recent studies indicate that, for the first time in modern history, we have a generation of people in their fifties and sixties who would like to remain vocationally active indefinitely. In fact, many will need to work to support their financial needs as they lack sufficient savings to provide them with an adequate retirement income. For the first time in our society, many will have to create a plan that ensures that they can work well into their seventies. For many people this is a very challenging dilemma. I personally see this situation as a great opportunity to find careers that can keep us active and extend our lives. Again, it's all in how we look at any potential challenge in our lives as well as our ability to look for opportunities we can benefit from.

Over the past few years, I have developed a new vision of the future. My vision of the future is a world of commerce in which we all remain contributing members for as long as we choose. Our lives will be enriched and extended because we have purpose. We will be living healthier lives because we are continuing to exercise our minds and emotions in a positive and productive manner. My vision is for everyone to take dominion over their career and to plan a future that will allow each one of us to control what we do and how long we continue to work, for the rest of our lives.

Getting back to my walk, half-way up the trail I wondered whether I could reach the top of the hill. I have been traveling quite a bit recently and I am slightly out of condition as I have failed to take my regular walks. It seemed to me that the hill was steeper and the path was longer than I had remembered it to be. I considered turning around and taking a less challenging path, but I knew I needed to keep going. I also knew that the extra effort would be good for me.

As I continued up the hill, I thought about how hard I had worked, and how many hours each week I had invested in building our business. I thought about the number of times I had gotten out of bed at 4:00 in the morning to work on a project or complete a few tax returns. (Actually getting up was better than lying there in bed thinking about all of the work!) I thought about the many times we had developed plans to open new markets or offer new services, only to discover that changes in the economy or new tax laws had closed these doors, forcing us to go in new directions. Then I focused on what I wanted for my future and how I would need to prepare myself to achieve it.

We recently purchased a new home in the Virgin Islands. It sits high on a hill in St. Thomas, and has one of those million dollar views of the island and the surrounding islands. We have an acre of tropical trees and plants that are absolutely beautiful. I enjoy that special feeling when I sit on our terrace and view the ocean, and the little town of Charlotte Amalie.

I love to walk on one of the white sand beaches there and plan for the future. I find that I get much more work done in that environment even when I am only working three or four hours each day. I can't sit down for very long and do nothing. I might be able to learn to fish but I wouldn't be able to spend the whole day fishing or playing golf. I would be lost without some involvement in my business.

You see, I could never mentally retire. I must have something to create, something to focus on. Do you know how I feel? Can you see what I am dealing with, as I look to the future and consider what my life will look like in another seven years from now?

Some of us are in a position where we will never be faced with being laid off, or faced with an early retirement package. Others, less fortunate, will have to face forced early retirement, and confront what they will do with themselves if they are faced with this experience. Even those who are owners or partners in businesses will have to face measurable challenges as they plan for the future. As they grow older, they are going to want to turn over more and more of the management of their company to other people. They are going to need to trust these people to make decisions and train them to handle each and every area of professional service or management that they often feel only they can handle. These business owners will be wise to develop a plan that will increase their employees' authority and responsibility, and reward them financially for their contribution.

Another major issue in career planning can arise when we develop challenges with our health. One of the best examples I have witnessed of a successful transition due to health challenges is how Tom and Mary handled theirs. Tom is an architect who has designed many outstanding buildings in our community. When I first met Tom he was 55 and had developed a very successful one-man business. In the past, he had tried to hire productive employees, and even had a partner for a year or two but had concluded that he worked best by himself and preferred to spend his time creating new buildings instead of trying to manage others.

Tom was also a dedicated family man, living the good life and very involved in his church. His wife Mary worked part time as a volunteer teacher's aide and from time to time helped out at their church. When I first met them eight years ago, they were both in excellent health.

Several years later, Tom called me to announce that he was buying new software to create his architectural drawings and how challenging it was for him to begin doing all of his design work on a computer. He bought the new system and began the process of reorganizing his operations around his new software program. He was one of the first people to acquire one of the new 19-inch computer monitors, to enable him to enjoy the largest possible view of his layouts.

I also remember the first time Tom told me he was having trouble with his eyes. I thought to myself, what in the world would he do if he could no longer see. How can he design anything if he can't see what he is designing? About a year went by and one day, during a meeting to review their retirement plan, Tom asked me to help him determine what to do. His eyes were getting weaker and he was concerned that he would not be able to continue his career much longer. We met about a week later and started to develop the most important blueprint Tom and ever worked on. This blueprint would be used to build an early retirement plan. The plan would control their financial future as well has his mental health for years to come.

We started by listing what his options were and how each option would affect his family financially as well as what degree of predictable control he would have over each option. His primary options were: (1) to attempt to sell his business, and reinvest the proceeds in other assets that would provide adequate and predictable income; (2) hire additional employees and focus his time and energy on developing the business; or (3) bring in one or two junior partners and gradually turn over most of the operations of the business to them, and structure compensation agreements and expenses so that he could at least enjoy a reasonable income from their activities.

After reviewing several personal concerns, Tom chose to pursue the third option of bringing into the business one or two junior partners. Once this decision was made, we then shifted our conversation to defining what skills and administrative talents the potential partners would need to have to make the plan work. In order to get the clearest picture of what these skills and administrative talents should be, I recommended that we take a very close look at his clientele, and what we could learn about their particular project needs and business style.

We also looked at where he saw the current opportunities for client expansion and how he could develop more profitable projects. Of course, Tom also had to redefine what he would be doing in the business and how his contribution could affect the business. Take note that in order to develop our career transition plan, we must factor into the plan our clients and their specific needs, as well as additional opportunities.

During our next meeting, our planning shifted to where to look for potential partnership. We decided to focus on two directions: (1) checking out who was attending the local association, and (2) seeing who was looking for intern work. Often, recent graduates with degrees in architecture will look for internship opportunities if they are focused on continuing their education. We also decided to run an ad in the local paper to announce the new career opportunities in Tom's business.

Within six weeks, Tom met and selected the two people that would become so valuable to him in his career transition. We developed a list of policies and procedures for Tom to pass on to his new partner/employees, and developed new standards for quality control and customer communications. After about six months of working together, they all settled into an effective team and the business began to grow.

Two years after our initial planning meetings, I met with Tom for our annual meeting to review his progress. By that time Tom's eyesight had deteriorated to the point he had to hold documents only five inches from his eyes to be able to see them. But otherwise, Tom was in excellent financial and emotional shape, and was continuing to work 40 hours or more each week in the business. Tom had successfully orientated his two new partners into the business. Through the new team, he had been able to expand the business to the level that his income had actually increased, even though he had taken on a considerable financial commitment. By structuring their initial salaries with bonuses and profit sharing, each of them was prospering—contributing to a very positive and productive environment. In turn, Tom was investing his time building relationships with their clients and enjoying his business more than ever.

Of equal importance, Tom can now work in the business as many years as he chooses to work. He can also control how often he shows up and how many hours he works. He has achieved both financial security as well as control of his future through the actions he took at a time when his future was in question. Tom created his future through creative planning, and by building faith in himself and his plan. He let go of his attitudes about his past experiences with employees and partners, and created a new business model that is now working for himself and his partners.

During the last half of my walk, I had finally made it up the hill. I sat on a bench for a while looking at my options, and how beautiful and peaceful the lake was. I then began to think about how different it would be as I walked back down the hill. Some of my options seemed very difficult to achieve but I realized they would be worth the effort. We all know it is a lot easier coming down the hill than it is walking up the hill.

This is often the case when we are faced with challenges in our career. It's often harder to create and implement the plan than to work within it once it's in operation. However, as we move forward and the ball gets rolling, our lives get easier. I can picture pushing this big ball up the hill and working hard to keep it going in the direction I want it to go in. Then, just as I feel I can push it no farther, I achieve a breakthrough and my life begins to roll swiftly like the ball rolling down the hill.

Isn't that the way life often works? Sometimes it seems like we simply can't get things rolling, and then at other times everything moves along without any perceived effort on our part. But it isn't that simple, nor in reality does it work that way at all. We achieve this momentum through creating new alternatives, correcting areas that need correction, and completing areas that are no longer positive factors in our life.

I must close now and get ready to go out to dinner. I am writing this letter from Newport Beach and we have some great restaurants in this area. I hope you are enjoying life and taking care of your health. Find a good hill to walk up and get some good exercise.

Your friend always,

James

SECTION FIVE

Exploring Business Ownership

WHERE DID ALL THE
BRIGHT PEOPLE GO?

"A Case Study of a Failed Business Venture"

Dear Jeff:

I trust my letter finds you well and prospering. I enjoyed hearing from you and appreciate receiving the information you sent regarding the real estate development in Hawaii. We are all well and enjoying life. I am happy to hear that you have been studying the principles I have shared with you in the past and that you are applying them. Unfortunately, we are living in an age when many bright people who need them don't have access to them.

Where I live in Silicon Valley, the highways are crowded with smart people heading for jobs they hold in hundreds of companies that provide the world with a myriad of high-tech products and services most people can't even explain how they work. They create and distribute these products and services around the world.

However, due to major industry down-turns, thousands of these brilliant people are currently out of work. They are as smart this year as they were two or three years ago when they were a part of the "wonder group" that brought forth the new economy. They have incredible resumes, and many have excellent contacts around the high-tech world. What they don't have is job security—and a large number lack the knowledge and experience required to start their own business.

During the past two years, we have witnessed a meltdown in the dot.com world in Northern California. Many of these dot.com companies were founded by brilliant people with great ideas. Many analysts have already tried to dissect the meltdown and in the fast-paced world of financial news, this subject has been discussed and is now old news. So, I'm not going to try to tell you what went wrong here in Northern California, but I am going to tell you about Hans and Robert and their experience in following their dream to own their own business.

I first met Robert in 1996 when he approached our firm to assist him in developing his business plan for his new company. During our first meetings, Robert spent several hours explaining his software design. I must admit, he was so bright that I struggled to keep up with him as he explained how his technology would change the world of data management on the internet. This guy had graduated from Stanford with a Bachelor of Science degree and had completed his MBA at Santa Clara University, two well-respected universities. Further, Robert had worked for two large companies for seven years gathering the knowledge critical to his ability to converse with other experts in his field. He was well qualified to take his design to the market place and had saved about $500,000 to seed his dream.

Two months into our relationship, Robert introduced me to Hans. Hans was another bright guy who had made several million dollars marketing technology products for one of the giant companies in Europe. Hans was from Germany, and he, his wife and two children were living the good life in one of the exclusive communities in the Bay Area. Hans was the million dollar man Robert needed to launch his marketing plan. He also was dedicated to becoming a successful business owner.

For the next thirty days, Robert, Hans and I met every week to review the assignments I had given each of them to lay out their blueprint for organizing their business. They were progressing well and I was beginning to see signs that they would be able to handle the operations of their business. You see, there is a vast difference between being technically bright and having the knowledge and skills to survive in the world of commerce. Robert was a ferocious reader and constantly referred to case studies he had read about as we talked about determining their job descriptions, and the team they would need to develop to pull off their dream.

Because their ultimate goal was to take their business public as soon as possible, Robert and Hans decided to talk with several local venture capital companies to find out what they thought about their business plan. Over the next month, I was fascinated as I witnessed their transformation triggered by their conversations with the Sand Hill Road power brokers.

In the event you are not familiar with our local venture capital world, we have numerous firms who have seeded the explosion of technology in Silicon Valley who have located their offices in an area on Sand Hill Road in Menlo Park, California. The decision-makers in these venture capital firms have negotiated a significant percentage of the capital development that has transformed Silicon Valley into one of the premier high tech business communities in the world.

These movers and shakers have made many multi-millionaires through their decisions which control who gets the gold and who doesn't. I can respect their contribution to commerce and certainly do not label them as a negative factor in the world of commerce. However, many people who have taken this path have learned a hard lesson regarding how this exclusive and high-stakes method of financing has affected their financial and business freedom.

Back to my story about Robert and Han's transformation. As they continued to talk with the power brokers, whose input was being listened to now carefully, Robert and Hans decided that their business plan was to make a "killing" on the initial public offering. They had perhaps unknowingly begun to take their eyes off of the core issue, which was the steps needed to build a solid business. Now, this reminds me to tell you now one of the most important principles of planning. This principle is to make all of your decisions with the end in mind. So, it appears that for Robert and Hans, "making a killing" had becoming the end in mind for their planning.

As we continue with this case study, you will want to remember that Robert and Hans' life began to change the day they shifted their focus from the value they could bring to the market place, to how much money they could make. Sure, we all want to become financially successful and yes, I wanted both of them to focus on the steps they would need to take to build a profitable business. But what we earn from our labor always follows effective and productive management. This is actually the theme of this case study of Robert and Hans and their venture into the world of owning their own business.

I remember the day Robert announced that we needed to abort our planning sessions until he could find two additional elements the venture capitalists wanted in their plan. They said these "elements" were necessary to position their company for a public offering. The first new element was they needed to recruit and hire a Chief Executive Officer who had a successful track record with a company who had made it through the public offering experience. Secondly, they needed to invest another $3,000,000 to finance the level of sales projected to place them in the "A" group for public offerings. Robert enthusiastically committed his energy to finding these new ingredients which, when added to the plan, would ensure that they would achieve their goal.

If you will remember, Robert and Hans had talked with several venture capital firms and finally found one who was interested in their proposal. However, this company was placing on them the two new requirements to participate in taking their company public. Robert and Hans were now very excited. After adding a Chief Executive Officer and infusing an additional $3,000,000 into the company, they asked if I would increase the figures on the proforma income and expense statement to project substantially higher sales and profit projections. Robert's comment was that they had to increase the income projections, so that the venture capital firm could bring the capital to the project and provide them with the best positioning to make them the most attractive candidate for a public offering.

During the next two meetings, Robert and Hans proceeded to stretch their sales projections to the limit and spent most of my time exploring where they could get their hands on another $3,000,000. They talked about "angels," bringing in new additional equity partners and how they could find a bank who would loan them the money so they could move forward.

I should interject that the reason they needed another $3,000,000 was because they would have to hire several more people including the proposed CEO. They had been told this would help them appear to be a more viable company in the eyes of their investors. They had to appear as a well-organized business with adequate staff to handle the projected sales.

It was at this point that I asked Robert and Hans to look at a business principle that I have found valuable from my experience in working with hundreds of business start-ups. The principle is that one must be able to have measurable goals and a realistic ability to achieve them. Goal-setting is valuable, but one must be able to establish goals which they have the highest probability of achieving. To set a goal is not, in itself, the most important part of the equation. Of equal importance is to have absolute faith and confidence that you can and will achieve the goal.

Robert was the first one to comment on my input. I remember his words as though he spoke them yesterday. He said, "The people at Sand Hill Road know what they are doing. They have made multi-millionaires of several people and they believe we can pull this off. We can time our public offering within the next 18 to 24 months. Let's focus on finding the CEO we will need. I'm sure he can help us raise the money we will need." For his part, Hans was focused on marketing issues and added that he believed they could achieve their new sales projections after gaining the involvement of his contacts in Europe. My two friends Robert and Hans had just lost control of their dream.

It doesn't matter whether your dream is to take a company public or establish your own small consulting firm. It doesn't matter whether you have $30,000 or $3,000,000 in capital to get you started. What matters is that you limit your initial resource plan to the capital, equipment and personnel that can get you to the first level of stability.

Although the level varies with different businesses, what this means is that you must determine what level of customers and revenues are necessary to cover your basic expenses and reserves, and generate a return on your investment. Once you reach this level in your new venture, you will then have the ability to accelerate to the next level of growth with dramatically increased probability you will achieve it. It is always wise to learn to walk before you run.

Robert and Hans had just sealed their fate in another important area that applies to every one of us regardless of the dream we have for owning and participating in our own business. Here is what happened over the following two months. The first challenge came in the form of a gentleman I will refer to as Roland. Of course that was not his real name, but Roland was referred to Robert by one of the partners in the venture capital firm as the CEO candidate who had the experience to make things happen. When I was first met Roland, I remember thinking to myself that this guy will chew up Robert and Hans and spit them out in little pieces the moment he takes control of the steering wheel of this company. Roland had an opinion about everything and seldom listened to anyone else's for longer than about ten seconds.

Roland was going to reshape the company for quick growth, and he had several friends he would bring into the company if Robert and Hans would agree to meet their salary requirements. Roland was going to be "easy" on them and would agree to become the Chief Executive Officer for a salary of only $285,000 per year for the first two years. In addition, he wanted to be guaranteed that he would receive 10% of the company stock immediately and another 10% prior to the company going public. Robert and Hans were so taken by his aggressiveness that they did not hesitate to agree to his demands and within a few days the company was officially formed and Roland took over as the captain of this new ship.

Following the activities to turn the "ship" over to Roland, our new leader came to Robert and Hans with one of his buddies, a banker by the name of Jim. Jim said he would help them arrange for a credit line at his bank. All they had to do was to personally pledge their stock and provide a personal guarantee to the bank. In exchange for this demonstration of confidence and commitment in their new venture, the bank would provide them with a $3,000,000 line of credit. Of course, the credit line would be reviewed every six months. Lunch that day was on the banker, but it eventually cost Robert and Hans their homes and their stock.

I am not telling you stories about peoples' challenges in starting business or their business failures to suggest that you should not venture into the world of commerce. They are not told to insinuate that bankers and venture capitalists are bad guys. I am sharing these experiences with you to tell you what to watch out for as wisdom comes from experience. Seldom do we have someone who can guide us through the new experiences as we venture out into the world of commerce.

I love owning my own business. I love the freedom it gives me and of equal importance, knowing that I can control the set of the sail of our ship. I would never consider taking our company public, because I do not want to be a servant to anyone on this planet. To be free we must become secure in ourselves, and then interdependent with other people with whom we can create win/win relationships. To be free, we must avoid selling ourselves out—which means we must do everything possible when forming a new business to keep our personal assets separate. It is important to avoid the trap of pledging personal assets to secure business obligations.

I understand where bankers are coming from, and I support the principle that we should take responsibility for our debts, but I cannot support any system that places its clients into positions of long-term servitude. Unfortunately, this is where millions of people in our society now find themselves. They are servants to the banks taking their interest every month—which in many cases is all or almost all of the monthly payment.

It's time to wind up my story about Robert and Hans. I want to share something important with you. As an advisor, I never attempt to tell clients what to do. I never want to rob them of the gift we all have which is the gift of choice. As I participated in the events that followed our luncheon with Jim the banker, there were several times I wanted to pull Robert and Hans aside and give them a good shaking.

You know how you feel when someone is being self-destructive and they don't see at all that they have a challenge? I wanted to challenge them to take back their company and focus on the importance of bringing their product to the marketplace instead of all of the positioning. I wanted them to focus on delivering the technology they had created to the marketplace. However, what they wanted to achieve was driving them, or more correctly stated, was controlling them.

In the months to follow, Robert and Hans violated two more important principles for starting a business and ended up losing ownership in their company and a lot more. For, as I alluded to earlier in my story, both were forced to sell their homes to pay down on their bank loan. What principles were at stake here? First, Robert and Hans violated the principle to take every step possible to build your business around the relationship between your present level of preparation and the specifically-identified opportunity.

What a strange and yet powerful principle. Some equate it to being at the right place at the right time but if we look at the principle closer, we will find that the important ingredient is that we must be able to take advantage of the opportunity.

We must be prepared to meet the opportunity with the knowledge, skills, talents and resources we have in that exact window of time. For Robert and Hans, there was an opportunity to start slowly and build a business around their then initial state of preparation. However, they lost their opportunity because they did not understand or apply this principle.

Between the two of them, Robert and Hans already had the skills and talents to take the business to the first level of stability and profitability.

Without bringing anyone else into their company and without borrowing additional capital, they could have launched their business and built a solid foundation for future growth. However, what they did was waste both their time and money which they promptly spent on unproductive activities. They lost their timing for entering the market and they lost control of sound budget planning. Due to poor planning, they chose to establish milestones they simply could not achieve.

When they hired Roland, Robert and Hans violated perhaps the most overlooked principle when starting a new business. This principle is one that sailors know well. It isn't the gale; it's the set of the sail that controls your direction. They simple lost control of their ability to manage their company and the direction they needed to take to survive the winds of economic change—change that has swept through our community and affected the lives of many bright people.

In contrast, another of our clients, Julie (who you may remember from a previous conversation) made it through the storm successfully and today is a successful human resources consultant. She was prepared to meet the needs of growing companies who have elected to outsource the management of their human resource department to an outside consultant. Julie was able to borrow enough money from her aunt, who had just sold a rental property and agreed to help out her niece with the gains she had achieved.

So where have all the bright people gone? You might think they have all gone to positions of importance and success, because we read about a few of them succeeding. Of course, this is hardly the case. Some, like Julie, have weathered the storm successfully while others like Robert and Hans, are still struggling to put the pieces back together.

There are many bright people in our community who are eager to succeed in their chosen field and might well achieve it, if only they would take the time and apply the principles to build a sound business. I have never met anyone who, in their own way, was not bright. Each and every person has something to contribute to our society—and you certainly deserve recognition for your contribution.

Certainly, some of the bright people will emerge in the future as great business owners, and others will grow to achieve measurable leadership in these companies. I know this is true because I know it is all a part of the ongoing process of change which will either support you in becoming stronger, or contribute to financial and business disappointments.

Take time now to focus on yourself and your talents and skills. Take time to examine where you want to be in your career in five years, where you want to be in ten years, and choose to change those areas where you currently see lack of opportunity and lack of the ability to win. For you to achieve becoming a winner does not have to mean that someone else will become a loser. Winning can produce wins for others, if you can focus in on where and how you can best contribute.

I must close now as we are having a dinner party for several of our friends. I wish you could be here with us tonight. I enjoy writing to you and I am happy you are enjoying my stories. I certainly enjoy yours. I trust you will have a great week, and I look forward to hearing about how you are progressing with your goals.

Your friend always,

James

XXIV

COULD YOU SEE YOURSELF IN YOUR OWN BUSINESS?

"Owning a Franchise May Enhance Your Chances for Success"

Dear Jeff:

I trust my letter finds you well and prospering. I am well and enjoying the process of establishing our new headquarters in Southern California. I hope you can come and see the new building in Irvine soon. In many ways, Irvine is emerging as the heart of the business world for this area.

Since we last spoke, I have been focusing on reviewing your thoughts about your career. I know you are examining your options and that you are looking at what will provide you with the greatest opportunity for success. This may be the time to examine if you would consider owning a franchise. Owning a franchise has proven to be an excellent career path for a number of our clients, and we are always looking to identify solid opportunities in that area of commerce. In fact, we are now preparing to develop a number of new franchise programs from our Economic Development Company in St. Thomas.

The business world can certainly be a very fascinating arena. Last night I had dinner with Ronald, a good friend and client. Ronald owns businesses in Switzerland, Russia and the United States. You might call him an entrepreneur, a real visionary in his field. I love seeing Ronald because we sit and talk about his latest ventures involving the Internet and emerging technology. He lives in Zurich and Moscow, and we often meet in Switzerland to enjoy our common interests and experience his culture.

During dinner, we spent about three hours catching up on the latest in our lives since I last saw him in Geneva. We talked about his experiences with his Russian operations and the world of franchising. My first experience in organizing a franchise was back in 1986. I knew little about the subject and had no idea how it would serve as such a successful career path for those who had worked in corporate America for years. The vast majority of these people had never seen themselves as business owners until they investigated the world of franchising.

I am sure that many people probably associate the term "franchising" with McDonalds, or one of several pizza franchises, but actually, one of the largest franchising operations in the world is General Electric. GE has numerous business units operating under its trade name and operating system. There are also franchises available that offer professional services such as business consulting and tax preparation.

Last night, Ronald and I began talking about utilizing the franchising structure to develop and operate a number of professional services centers throughout Europe. In Europe alone, we calculated that we could create over 1,000 new business units over the next five years. This represents 1,000 new business outlets that would be owned and operated by 1,000 people who will be provided with a business format that has an 80% probability for business survival.

Statistics show that for every ten people who acquire a franchise, more than 80% are still in business after five years. Compare this to the statistics that state that 70% of the new business startups will have failed within five years. This certainly raises the question as to why the often overlooked world of franchising holds the key to providing individuals with an opportunity to achieve greater career security—which so many people are struggling to achieve in their lives.

Getting back to our dinner last night, I was fascinated to learn from Ronald that the technology we would use in Europe and the United States would include a new technology he called "blade technology." Through blade technology, Ronald said that all we had to do to add capacity to our server was to add another small "blade" to the box. Each time we added another blade, we could host another 1,000 clients' websites on our server. We could literally service all of Europe and all of the U.S. on two small metal boxes that would take up less than 800 square feet of space. In addition, the new concept along with additional technology could effectively cut consumer costs by 50%—which would certainly be valuable for developing new customers. All we need to do now is to find 1,000 people with the interest and energy to be in business with us and provide them with the processes and systems to build their business through our franchise program in their communities.

The point of this illustration is that instead of one company expanding throughout the world by establishing offices and hiring its own employees, the business would be expanded through granting licenses to several thousand people. These license holders will then be able to enjoy the unique experience and job security that can come from owning and operating their own business within a sound business format.

Every year, thousands of people leave their jobs to build their economic and job stability through acquiring a license to operate one of the several thousands of franchised business throughout the world. What they acquire is the right to utilize an organized business format that guides them to open and operate a business. The franchisor has taken the steps to develop the business format so as to operate the business to achieve the highest level of effectiveness and efficiency, as well as provide a trade name that offers valuable name recognition and assistance in developing clients. The franchisor also provides both initial and ongoing training and supervision to improve the probability that the new business owner will have the opportunity to establish a solid operation and build a profitable business.

The franchisor must also continue to stay abreast of changes in technology and conduct research to ensure that the business format will remain competitive, and continue to meet the needs of its target customer. This system provides licensees with both the support and the opportunity that may not be present if they attempt to start their own business.

After dinner, Ronald and I took a walk to help burn off the calories from the steaks we had just enjoyed and to talk about the best candidates for operating these franchises. I asked Ronald who he would offer the licenses to in Germany and Italy where he will initially launch the business. He stated that he would contact companies who wanted to expand their services, and show them the benefits of establishing additional revenues by acquiring a license to operate our franchise in their community. He stated that those companies would in turn hire employees to market the service. Ronald then asked me who we should offer the licenses to in the U.S. My recommendation was that we offer the licenses to individuals who are considering a change in their career. We would also offer this opportunity to those recently laid off and who are tired of the feeling of insecurity that can arise from not knowing how long their next job might last.

Each time we experience a business cycle that creates layoffs and business failures, we find that a number of people respond by buying their own business or franchise. Over time, those who become franchise owners learn that their job security lies in their ability to perform the requested service through the business format. They also learn and that there was no real security from their previous status as an employee. Most of those who have made the transition from employee to operating their own business admit how frightened they were when they first focused on life without a "guaranteed" paycheck every month. In time, however, they grew to have confidence in their ability to generate ongoing business and predictable income.

From time to time, I meet someone who has had an undesirable experience in the world of franchising. From these discussions, I have found three primary reasons owning a franchise did not work for them. The first reason is that they acquired a franchise that did not or could not meet their income needs. If an individual needs to generate a certain level of cash flow every week to meet their financial obligations, they should not make a career change that will create additional financial challenges. You can minimize financial risks through a comprehensive investigation of each franchise opportunity, and establish whether or not you should acquire a new or an existing license.

There are several reasons to acquire an existing franchise. But the most important one is to be able to acquire a business with sufficient cash flow to meet your income needs. When opening a new location, it is possible that the unit may not generate needed income for quiet some time which will create a challenge in those situations.

The second issue that can create challenges from owning a franchise is that the business format is incompatible with your intellectual needs and vocational skills. This can lead to boredom and frustration.

The third challenge resulting in an undesirable experience from owning a franchise is when the business requires that you hire and supervise a number of employees. New franchisees may lack the interest or maturity to manage employees which also can result in frustration and poor results. One example of this challenge is attempting to operate a restaurant wherein large numbers of employees are required to keep the franchise running smoothly.

If you have decided to examine new options to the world of franchising, I recommend that you begin with the end in mind. Start by researching the different types of businesses currently offering franchise licenses, and match these businesses with your passions, talents and skills. Determine exactly what type of business you would enjoy and if you want others in your family to be involved in the business with you.

The next step would be to gather information from all of the franchising companies offering licenses in your community that interest you. Take time to talk with other franchisees to get a clear and hopefully objective picture of what to expect from ownership of one of their licenses. Avoid getting caught up in others' problems and opinions, and focus on the core issue, which is how effective the business format is for developing and servicing the clients. Also verify the scope of the franchisor's training program and level of ongoing support. Of course be sure to verify that the product or service offered is what it is promoted to be.

The third step is to evaluate whether or not it is best for you to start a new unit, or acquire an existing unit. People sell their licenses for numerous reasons, and acquiring an existing unit may prove to be your best path to business ownership. Once you have determined that you wish to purchase an existing location, work with an experienced broker to represent your interests whether you are dealing with the franchisee or directly with the franchisor. Of course, you may determine that the best path for you is to open a new location. This can be an excellent decision if you want to reduce your initial capital outlay and experience what it's like to open a new location.

The fourth step is to establish a thorough financial plan before you venture into the world of business ownership. Your financial analysis must include the most effective way to finance your new business, and when you will be able to resume making contributions to your retirement accounts.

Perhaps you can also discuss your plans with your children as they could benefit from participating in the franchise with you. I know you wish the best for them and want them to discover a career that can provide them with the security we all strive to find in our lives. I have also observed that many people wish they could spend more time with their children, and be able to contribute more in their search to learn how life works. I have enjoyed working with my daughter for eight years now, and can tell you that it has been a wonderful experience for me.

Many people have enjoyed the benefits from inviting their children to work with them in their business. It provides both parties with an excellent way to make agreements with each other, and experience what effective teamwork is all about. Others simply enjoy having their family with them, and knowing that the business can continue to grow and prosper regardless of their level of participation. Getting your family involved in your business can be an intelligent and rewarding experience and is highly recommended.

We are often fascinated by the success stories of entrepreneurs who have taken their idea and created a successful business with it. We can only dream of achieving such success. We may wonder how it is that we are not able to discover those ideas that would benefit the world and make us an overnight success. Through the years, I have had numerous people come to me with ideas they felt they could build a business around. I remember one gentleman who had invented a new tool for picking up trash along the freeway. He told me that he had spent years thinking about how he could take his idea to the marketplace and make enough money to enable him to quit his job. But he lacked the ability to become an entrepreneur as he could not take his idea to any new level to organize it into a product or conceive how to market it.

Don't worry if you feel that you are not cut out to be an entrepreneur. Refocus on how you could enjoy becoming a business owner through acquiring the rights to operate a business that someone else has created and organized to the point where there are solid and effective processes you can follow to be successful. Don't worry about trying to invent the next wheel. Let someone else do that and focus on how you can change your life through acquiring an existing wheel someone else has already engineered. The challenge is to find a business that runs smoothly and will take you down the road to financial and career freedom.

In previous letters, we have talked about how our emotional centers can affect us and limit our ability to grow and prosper. What I want to remind you of is that your current emotional center can block you from discovering the benefits of franchise ownership. Many people believe that their importance and security is in their job title. Being a project manager or assistant vice president provides them with a sense of belonging and importance. Others have centered their feeling of worth in their level of education. They position their PhD or MBA designation as the basis for their security and would hesitate to purchase a McDonalds franchise due to what they believe others would think about them as an MBA owning a hamburger restaurant. It is important to avoid getting lost in a false world of perceived security, or failing to allow yourself to move forward into a new world of different titles and designations due to old feelings of importance.

I encourage you to open your mind to the possibility of achieving financial and career security through franchise ownership. I am going to close this letter now as I must prepare for a staff meeting but I will be writing again soon. Take care of yourself and give my warmest regards to everyone in your family. I look forward to our next conversation.

Your friend always,

James

SECTION SIX

Envisioning Our Mission for the Future

XXV

Can We Isolate Ourselves from All of the Turmoil Around Us?

"Looking Again at the Principles for Peace and Strength"

Dear Friends:

I trust my letter finds you well and enjoying life. I am traveling more now between our offices in Northern and Southern California and enjoying life. I have thought about several letters I have written to each of you and your letters to me. Although none of you know each other, we all have one thing in common which is that we are all focused on strengthening ourselves and achieving ongoing peace in our lives.

As we have communicated to each other over the past few years, we have all witnessed a growing amount of turmoil. The news has been dominated lately by reports of increased political unrest and economic turmoil. Hardly a day goes by that we are not reminded how our retirement accounts have dwindled in value due to challenges in the stock market. Nations are at war with each other, with virtually no sign of finding peaceful solutions. Corporations continue to lay off more people, leaving more and more people out of work and watching their personal debt skyrocket. Several of our major corporations have lost their image of strength and security through their failure to understand the law of sowing and reaping, and many of our politicians are recommending solutions that only reduce our ability to take control of our lives.

With all of this turmoil around us, can we isolate ourselves from it and find a safe haven where we can enjoy peace and security? Based on my experience and the feedback I have received from clients who have applied the principles I have been applying, the answer is absolutely yes.

I have shared a few of the principles we have been given to support you in building your life on a solid foundation. I have not written to give you false hope, nor to share ideas that only work some of the time or for some of the people. These principles can assist us in withstanding any storm that may come through our lives. They will help you as you begin your personal journey to isolate yourself from all of the turmoil around you. I want you and your family to enjoy greater peace and to know that the principles have been given to us through love and through grace.

We do not have to understand everything to find peace, nor do we have to earn it through anything we have to prove to anyone. Once you have it, no one can take it from you. Once you have filled your mind and emotions with this peace, you will never again have to return to feelings of fear and insecurity that plague millions of people around us.

Through love, we find intimacy and through intimacy we find passion. The moment we become passionate about applying the principles is the moment we begin to isolate ourselves from all of the turmoil around us. People around us will begin to see us differently and they too will want to learn from us and hopefully be more open to discover peace for themselves.

We can also empower our children with our peace and we can build strong personal relationships with it. We can emerge as leaders in our community and unlock our innate purpose through finding peace and confidence. All we need to do to begin our journey is to choose to have faith and confidence in the principles I have shared with you. Our journey begins with choice.

As I look back on my life, I can see numerous examples of my failure to apply the principles and the poor results that followed from failing to apply them. However, the past is gone and the future is what we make of it. We can start over at any time and build our lives from this point forward on a solid foundation. We can break free of anything that weakens us, and we can correct or complete any relationship that is not in highest purpose. All we need to do is to choose to let the past go and concentrate on creating a new future.

I invite you to consider something for a moment. Consider if everything in life is in order, and unfolding through our lives due to God's principles, or if life is based on random experiences with no chance for any of us to control anything. Is there a guide, or do we simply live and die with no one we can have absolute confidence in? When you examine your own position about whether or not there really is a Supreme source of wisdom and knowledge, do you have absolute certainty that your position is true?

I have an important request of you. My request is to determine where your source of knowledge and wisdom lies if you haven't already done so. Determine who and what you rely on and who and what you have absolute faith in? Then determine who and what you have absolute confidence and absolute trust in? Before you go any further in reading this letter, I ask you to answer these questions. Thank you for taking the time to take this step. I acknowledge you for honoring my request.

Let's move forward now to examine what specific steps to take to isolate ourselves from all of the turmoil around us. Let's make sure we know what to do when we see the turmoil or when we feel it inside ourselves. Turmoil is a lot like storms that come and go during the year. We never know when they will come but we always know when they arrive. I have examined experiences I have had in the past with a number of clients who were able to eliminate turmoil from their life. I asked myself what each one of these people did that started their lives moving in a new direction? What they did was to apply the one thing no one can take away from us. They chose to quit reacting and chose a new direction. What they did was to apply the power of choice. So the first step you can take is to choose to change.

It only takes a split second to choose to go in a new direction. It only takes a second to decide that we will no longer be a part of the turmoil swirling around us. Once you have chosen to go in a new direction, then determine where the turmoil is coming from. Examine each situation to determine where the other person is coming from, and whether or not you can do anything about it. As an example, there is little I can do about the situation in the Middle East but take it to prayer. Since there is nothing else I can do about that source of turmoil, then I simply choose not to be a part of it.

Many times the turmoil is the result of relationships in our family. I know someone who has a difficult parent living with her. The parent has a deep-seeded need to control and is very unhappy with herself. Both her need for control and her unhappiness spills out onto her daughter, and everyone else in the household. The parent's behavior creates turmoil and often creates feelings of frustration and even guilt in other family members because they feel they should always love and accept their parent's behavior no matter what they do or say.

My friend finally chose to correct this situation and asked if there were steps she could take to achieve peace with her mother. If you are having a similar experience with a parent or a child, you can appreciate how frustrating this situation can be. When dealing with a member of your family, there are three initial steps you can take to start the process for achieving peace in each situation. These steps were recommended to my friend to take action in her situation:

1. Begin the process of healing by presenting to the other person a clear statement of what you need and what you want to achieve. Avoid referring to the situation as a problem and avoid statements that include the word you in them. Saying "you have" or "you did" will only place the other person on the defensive which will trigger their automatic need to defend themselves and they will no longer be listening to you.

   In this conversation, you want to focus on telling them how you feel, what you want and what you are willing to do to achieve your goal. When you conduct your conversation, be sure that the other person is not presently dealing with any upset. In other words, make sure that they are calm, not into reaction about anything and that they are willing to listen to you. You can arrange for the visit by simply asking them if they have a few minutes to listen to something that is important to you. That is all you need to say.

   When you meet with the individual, let them know immediately that there is an issue that you are dealing with that you want to resolve. Then tell them how you feel about the situation, what you want, and what you are willing to do to achieve it. When you present your message, you shouldn't have any challenge calmly expressing how you feel and what you want. However, you may want to think carefully about what you are willing to do before you say it. The reason is that you must be willing to do exactly what you say you are going to do.

So, take the time to think through the entire situation and be sure you know what you are going to do if the other person chooses not to honor your request.

Now I want to tell you about the next step to take. It is to deliver your presentation and then be quiet. Let me repeat this step because it is very important. When you have stated how you feel, what you want to achieve, and what you are willing to do, then quit talking and do not say a word until after the other party responds to your request. What you hear next is very important. What you will hear is how they see the situation and what they are willing to do about it. Listen very carefully to their answer and see if you can determine where they are coming from with their behavior. Here lies the opportunity to determine what the problem is and how they feel about it.

If the other party is willing to meet your needs, then make an agreement with them. Ask the other person to repeat the agreement so that you can be sure they understand what they are agreeing to. Then thank them for listening to you and end the conversation. The goal to be achieved in this step is to correct the situation.

2. If the other family member takes a defensive position or states that this is the way they are and you will simply have to accept them, then you have a new decision to make. You will then need to decide whether or not you will complete the relationship as it currently exists by requesting that they leave your home or perhaps terminate their visit.

When you have to focus on this decision, it is very important to be sure that you are completely free of fear or guilt. If you are dealing with a child who is too young to leave the household, obviously you must have a different action plan. But in the case of a parent or older child, you do have options and one that will most always work within the situation.

If you ask them to leave, be sure to let them know that they are more than welcome back in your home when they decide to honor your request. It is important to remember that by taking this step, you will demonstrate to the other party your strength and resolve, and this alone may often motivate the other person to respect you and your request.

3. The third step to take is to make sure that you have given the child or parent completely and totally to God. This step is important because we often allow ourselves to take positions in our relationship with others that are not in highest purpose for the growth of either party. It is better for a loved one to learn a lesson than to live their life in weakness or to go on through live treating others in a manner that is not in highest love or highest purpose. We may feel responsible for someone else and often make decisions from feelings of sorrow or fear. Also, do not lose faith in the other person to finally choose to change and correct their behavior. But, while you are waiting for them to change, it is not necessary to subject yourself and other family members to the challenging family member's behavior.

I have seen several dysfunctional families as well as numerous dysfunctional businesses. As I have already stated, we can take action to heal these situations through choice. I have already shared three principles to apply whenever we are faced with turmoil in our family or in our company. These principles are that we "create" a new solution, "correct" the existing situation, or "complete" the relationship. Remember the three "C's" as they will assist you in eliminating turmoil from your life.

Many of us have grown up in an atmosphere of global unrest and some have been affected by the various wars that have been fought over the past 60 years. Today, we are facing a new kind of global unrest as it has become a war not of governments fighting governments but a war driven by spiritual hate and resentment. The present conflict presents an altogether different situation, because it has no borders nor does it have the usual political objectives. It is more likely that this type of war will be of far greater emotional impact to everyone involved and we are all exposed to this turbulence whether we like it or not.

There is nothing you or I can do about this conflict, but to ask God to protect us and our families from it. We can only choose to overcome our fear and stand on our faith that our families will escape the violence.

We have talked about financial turmoil and I know that you have told me how important financial security is to you. I also know that you want to make sure that your children grow to enjoy their own financial security. I am often reminded of the fact that we always reap the seeds we sow and it takes time to see a crop grow. Farmers know this and wait patiently until they are ready for the harvest of the seeds they planted months ago. We should remind ourselves daily that our financial security is a product of the seeds we sow and the habits we apply to the management of our money. We are also wise to teach our children these principles.

I gave a presentation yesterday to a number of people on the subject of six mistakes people make in managing their long-term savings. Most of the people in the audience listened intently during the presentation. Toward the end of my talk, a few of them began to participate in the seminar and started to ask questions and give their point of view. What struck me about their comments was that most of them were caught up in what had happened to them over the past year. Their entire point of view was based on how well they had managed their money during that short period of time.

In order to have peace in our financial life, we must keep our eyes on our plan and where we are going. We must focus on what we must do each month to follow the principles that will strengthen our ability to achieve financial security. And, we must have confidence and faith that we will achieve our goals.

I woke up this morning and thanked God for my career and for the abundance in my life. I am so thankful that twenty years ago I took the time to examine why I was here and what my mission was. I am thankful that I chose then to get rid of the areas in my business life that I didn't want and certainly didn't need. There is so much peace in knowing that we have the right career. It is not important to have a career that someone else wants you to have or simply take a job to ensure that you will be able to pay your bills.

There is peace and joy in knowing that we are in highest purpose. If God has a plan for us, then He has a plan for commerce. If you are in union with Him, then He has a plan for you that you can find if you will seek it. As I have shared with you before, start by making sure that you have chosen to be in highest purpose and then ask God where He sees you in His plan for commerce. You will find great peace from taking these steps and from discovering your purpose and passions. The most important principle for eliminating turmoil in our career is to be sure we have the right one.

We have talked about relationships and have both found that all great relationships are built on met needs and the principles for friendship. When we look at peaceful relationships, we find the following present: (1) Acceptance, (2) Willingness (3) Cooperation, (4) Enthusiasm, (5) Agreement, (6) Interest, (7) Attunement, (8) Oneness. When we examine relationships in turmoil we find: (1) Antagonism, (2) Anger, (3) Resentment, (4) Hostility, (5) Fear, (6) Worry and Guilt, (7) Indifference, (8) Separation. As we focus on building solid friendships, we find the secret is to eliminate the negative emotions and replace them with opposite positive emotions. Also, we should always remember that the principle elements of friendship are: (A) Acceptance, (B) Trust, (C) Respect, (D) Commonality.

We are able to eliminate turmoil as we work to build solid friendships with our personal and business partners by applying the principles we have been given.

I have shared with you that a number of years ago I was in great turmoil in my own life and couldn't seem to find peace no matter how much money I made or how many places I sought to find it. I looked in a number of places for the answer and watched others carefully to see if anyone else around me had found it. I watched people at my country club, and discovered that the majority of these people were in greater turmoil then I was. I looked at business associates and at members of my family and found that the only ones at peace were those who had a strong faith in God and sense of purpose in their lives. I didn't understand it but I knew it was true.

In looking back on that time in my life, I realize that my challenge was that I couldn't understand how others had achieved their peace because I simply didn't know God. Sometimes you can be around someone for years and not really know them. He or she may even be watching out for you but you are not seeing their protection or their love because you are focused on other things. I did not make my choice to get to know God in any church or synagogue. I did not make it out of fear or guilt. I made my choice one day while talking to someone who asked me if it was time for me to choose to be in highest purpose, truth, and love because these fundamentals would strengthen me and support me in receiving what I had asked for. I made my choice because I knew, deep inside, that it was time for me to choose and I knew that I was tired of trying to do things my own way.

When I think back on the day I made my choice, I remember my friend John saying to me that purpose strengthens and when we are not in purpose we are weakening ourselves. I remember John saying that truth strengthens and how important it was to discover God's truth, as our truths are often highly edited by our own feelings, emotions and belief system. I also remember when he said that love strengthens and we always find our peace in our love. I can verify how true that is. I cannot find the words to tell you how much these truths have affected my life.

When I made my choice, my life started to change and has been changing ever since that day as I have chosen to continue to grow in purpose, truth, and love. I have chosen also to expand my strength and my ability to achieve my mission as I have found my joy is in my love, and therein also lies a large portion of my intimacy and passion.

If you will take the first step, all the rest of the steps will become clear as it is time to take them. You will have peace with your present experiences. You will be able to have absolute confidence and absolute faith and trust in God and in yourself. Only then can you begin the process of aligning yourself with others who share your mission and your vision for your future. This will take care of improving your personal and business relationships as well as demonstrate to your children how God thinks and how He works to bring forth His plan while always providing each of us with the power of choice.

I must go now and prepare for the week ahead. I enjoy our talks and your letters. Communication is so important and it is wonderful to have friends who are seeking the same things in life that I am seeking for myself and my family. When I write again, I want to share my mission with you. I want to tell you where I am going and invite you to be a part of the mission.

Until then, I trust that each of you will focus on your own mission and develop your own plan for your future. We can then take a look at each other's dreams and goals for the future and be able to determine where we can best support each other. All good relationships are based on met needs and I am looking forward to discovering where I can be a part of meeting your needs.

Until my next letter, I leave you with one thought. Will we be the ones who turn things around in a world that appears to be out of control?

Your friend always,

James

ABOUT THE AUTHOR

Wm. James Long is President and a principal of Alliance Royale, a holding company that operates within the United States through Alliance Royale Advisory Centers, Portfolio Advisors Alliance and the Institute For Excellence. He has a distinguished background in the financial and business services industries. In this capacity, he has helped thousands of individuals to better manage their finances, businesses and life transitions throughout the United States and Europe.

Mr. Long has created twelve business formats that serve as the foundation for professional services provided by Directors at the Alliance Royale Advisory Centers, and his tenets provide the foundation of the Personal and Business Effectiveness Programs presented through the Institute For Excellence. He is a much sought-after speaker on topics of leadership and action planning.

In **THE CHALLENGE**, Mr. Long draws on his 35 years of business and life experience working with thousands of individuals to create, organize and manage financial and business plans.

THE CHALLENGE
QUICK ORDER FORM

If you enjoyed reading **THE CHALLENGE** and would like to order a copy
for a colleague, friend, or family member, simply complete this form
and **FAX** to: **(949) 442-6648**
You may also order online @ **www.allianceroyale.com**

Name: _____

Address: _____

City: _____ State: _____ Zipcode: _____

Phone: (_____) _____

Email: _____

Please check here if you'd like to be included on our mailing list for events in your area: ☐

QUANTITY YOU ARE ORDERING @ $22.95 _____ SUBTOTAL $ _____

Add 7.75% sales tax for all orders shipped within California $ _____

Shipping and Handling ➔ Waived If Ordered by April 1st, 2003 ___ N/C ___

AFTER APRIL 1st ➔ ADD $5.00 SHIPPING/HANDLING PER BOOK $ _____

TOTAL $ AMOUNT ENCLOSED FOR THIS ORDER $ _____

We accept the following forms of payment:
CHECK, MONEY ORDER and CREDIT CARD *(Check one)*

Check Enclosed ☐

Money Order Enclosed ☐

Please bill my Credit Card ☐

Please provide us with your Credit Card Information.
We accept VISA and MASTERCARD.   Expires (Month/YR)

MASTERCARD # _____

VISA # _____

Name As It Appears on Card: _____

Authorized Signature: _____

FOR OFFICE USE:	REF #303